A类 / G类通用

华研外语
TOPWAY ENGLISH

雅思语法

主　编：何国武

副主编：叶　彤

编　委：张芳芳　　刘晓君　　谭凯茵

杨宇畅　李琦琪

 中国出版集团有限公司　　 世界图书出版公司

懂方法 更有效
www.huayan-edu.com

前言 *PREFACE*

───────── 您在备考雅思时是否会遇到这些问题？ ─────────

- 雅思成绩 5 分以下，做真题错误太多，没提升
- 记了半年词汇，阅读文章还是看不懂
- 背了各种作文模板，写作分数还是在 5 分徘徊
- 多次参加考试反复刷分，却无法提分

如果您遇到以上问题，说明您的语法基础不扎实！为此，本书对症下药，专门讲解雅思阅读和写作中需要掌握的基础语法知识，并辅以针对性练习，考什么学什么，考什么练什么。解决语法根源问题，才能有效提分。

一　阅读篇：零基础看懂英文句子

➡ 14 节句法讲解 + 双语例句 + 单句拆分训练

　　本书摒弃传统语法书烦琐的语法体系，避开晦涩难懂的语法术语，针对性地解决看得懂单词，看不懂句子的问题。设置【真题句解读·实战演练】版块，指导考生利用简化、拆分等手段划分句子意群，提取出句子的关键信息，从而达到解题的终极目标！

　　每个句法点均配套对应的例句，在语境中学语法，便于理解和运用所学语法知识。且所有例句均选自雅思真题或与真题同等难度的句子，只学考试要用到的语法点，省时省力！

　　每个句法点后均有针对性的习题，以便即时检测学习成果，从简单句到复杂的长句，循序渐进，逐步达到看懂长难句的目的。

➡ 200 道真题句训练 + 图解难句 + 词汇注释

　　阅读篇第 3 章设有 200 道雅思单句训练，分为基础训练和提高训练，一页一练，并附有【词汇注释】，考生可免查词典，同步积累词汇。答案部分以图解方式分析句子成分，清晰易懂（如下图）。

5 The Massachusetts Institute of Technology	investigated	automated mobility	in Singapore.
主语	谓语	宾语	后置定语

【参考译文】麻省理工学院研究了新加坡的自动化出行情况。

【理解要点】本句的主语是 The Massachusetts Institute of Technology，谓语是 investigate 的过去式，后接宾语 automated mobility in Singapore，其中 in Singapore 是 automated mobility 的后置定语，说明是哪里的自动化出行情况。

二 写作篇：零基础写对英文句子

➡ 7 大常见错误

写作篇第 1 章总结了写作中常见的 7 大基础性错误，包括拼写、标点以及用词错误，帮助考生减少不必要的丢分。每一节后均附有改错、填空等针对性练习，提高考生对写作易错点的敏感度。

➡ 6 类组句方式

攻克基础性错误后，考生需要掌握组句方式，才能写出正确的句子。写作篇第 2 章讲解了 6 类在雅思写作中常用的基本句式，包括简单句、并列句、被动句、定语从句、名词性从句和状语从句，通过具体实例分析和相应的练习，帮助考生一步步写出语法正确的句子。

➡ 12 大写作技巧

根据语法多样性的评分标准，考生写出的句子仅仅做到没有语法错误是不够的，在此基础上，句子还要出彩，才能拿到高分。写作篇第 3 章分别从句式变换、同义改写和论证句型的使用三个方面讲解写作技巧，帮助考生从"写对句子"进阶到"写好句子"。

➡ 句子写作训练

写作篇第 4 章精选 150 个句子和 10 篇雅思例文，从基础到提高，训练考生综合运用写作语法点的能力。

三 视频精讲，解读真题句和写作语法点

阅读篇的【真题句解读·实战演练】和写作篇的第 2、3 章均附有配套视频，由一线雅思老师讲解，扫描内文和封底二维码即可获取，方便考生随时随地学习。

▶ 真题句解读·实战演练

在做雅思阅读时，实际上同学们并不需要将每个句子成分都分析透彻，**关键是要找准句子的谓语动词**。找到谓语动词，再根据谓语动词判断前后的成分，理解句子的基本结构即可。

例1 Composer David Cope invented a program called Experiments in Musical Intelligence, or EMI. 真

译1 作曲家大卫·柯普发明了一个名为"音乐智能实验"的程序，也称 EMI。

编 者

CONTENTS 目录

第 1 章 7大常见语法错误

一 注意拼写的统一

雅思写作中，采用英式或美式拼写都是可以接受的，并不影响分数，但这两种方式不能混用。

例 My favorite colour is red. ✗

My favourite colour is red. ✓（统一用英式拼写）

My favorite color is red. ✓（统一用美式拼写）

译 我最喜欢的颜色是红色。

二 字母拼写错误

英文字母的拼写主要注意以下几个问题：

①多写字母，特别是双写了不需要双写的字母。例如，writing误写成writting；process误写成proccess等。

②漏写字母，其中特别注意要双写的字母。常见的错误有government误写成goverment，漏掉n；currently误写成curently，漏掉r。

③字母顺序错误。例如，believe误写成beleive，society误写成soceity，receive误写成recieve等。

Tips

以下是剑桥学习者词库（Cambridge Learner Corpus）中最常拼错的10个单词，你能拼对吗？

1. goverment　　**2.** tempreture　　**3.** oppotunities　　**4.** countris　　**5.** excercise

6. nowdays　　**7.** competion　　**8.** droped　　**9.** happend　　**10.** diffrent

更多雅思写作中易拼错的单词，详见附录（pp. 110~111）

三 区分是一个单词还是两个单词

有些合成词是一个单词，中间没有空格，如：

countryside	lifespan	website	wildlife	workforce	workplace
undergo	outbreak	outcome	outside	overall	overcome
anybody	elsewhere	everything	someone	sometimes	furthermore
moreover	downtown	throughout	maybe(注意与may be区分)		

有些合成词中间要带有连字符，如：

make-up　　well-being　　twenty-four　　thirty-fifth

四 形近词误用

英文中有些单词的拼写非常接近，但语义差别却非常大，要特别注意不要混淆这类词汇。以下为一些常见的形近词：

quite 相当——quiet 安静的　　　　affect 影响（*v.*）——effect 结果，影响(*n.*)

adapt 适应——adopt 采用　　　　angel 天使——angle 角度

dairy 牛奶场——diary 日记

dessert 甜食——desert 抛弃(v.), 沙漠

sweet 甜的——sweat 汗水

later 后来——latter 后者

contact 接触——contract 合同

abroad 在国外——aboard 上(船，飞机)

except 除外——expect 期望

loose 松的——lose 丢失

area 区域——era 时代

vocation 职业——vacation 假期

casual 随便的——causal 表原因的

through 通过——though 虽然

Tips

如何提高单词拼写的准确率？

- 根据单词的拼写规律记忆单词。划分单词音节，了解常见的字母组合的发音，对于部分特殊的字母组合，多花时间进行标注和记忆。
- 多开口朗读单词。将说和记结合，提高对单词的熟悉度，提升单词的拼写准确度。
- 注意动词的不规则变化、动词的第三人称单数变化、名词的单复数变化等等。
- 写作完成后，检查自己的拼写错误。用本子记下经常拼错的单词，常背常记，避免在同一个单词上摔跤多次。

五 大小写错误

写作中要注意哪些情况字母需要大写，其中最关键的是以下几点：

① 句子第一个单词的首字母大写。

② I (表示"我")任何时候都大写。

③ 专有名词首字母大写。最典型的例子有国名(如 Germany、the United States、Britain)；地名(如 Paris、Beijing、Texas)；表示国籍、民族、宗教等的词(如 Chinese、South African、Buddhist)；机构名(如 the United Nations、the National Museum)；月份、星期(如 October、Monday)。

④ museum、university、station、hospital 等词如果是机构或建筑名称的一部分，首字母要大写，反之则不需要大写。

⑤ 季节名称(spring、summer、autumn、winter)不需要大写。

⑥ 一些首字母缩略词需要全部大写，如 AIDS、COVID-19、CD 等。

例1 Then **I** went to the **University of Krakow**.

译1 之后我去了克拉科夫大学上学。

例2 **I** plan to go to **university** in the future.

译2 我计划将来要上大学。

例3 According to an expert at the **Natural History Museum** in **London**, ...

译3 据伦敦自然历史博物馆的一位专家所言，……

例4 All **museums** and art galleries should be free because they are important parts of a country's culture.

译4 所有博物馆和美术馆都应该免费开放，因为它们是国家文化的重要组成部分。

缩写(contraction)是指单词缩写成带撇号(')的形式。正式学术论文一般不使用缩写形式。雅思写作属于正式文体，所以不建议同学们在作文中使用缩写，如hasn't应写成has not，还有can't应写成cannot。

[例] Even though many people **don't** like change, it is inevitable throughout everyone's life. ✗

Even though many people **do not** like change, it is inevitable throughout everyone's life. √

[译] 即使很多人不喜欢改变，但这是每个人一生中不可避免的事情。

小试牛刀

Exercise 1　改正下列单词的拼写错误。

1. dissappear _____ 2. througout _____

3. benificial _____ 4. knowlege _____

5. tecnology _____ 6. ambulence _____

7. travle _____ 8. offical _____

9. recomend _____ 10. nutrion _____

11. kindergarden _____ 12. polution _____

13. universety _____ 14. wether _____

15. orgin _____

Exercise 2　圈出下列句子中拼写错误的单词，并改正。

1. Children can easily be influenced by advertments.

2. Tourism can damage local culture and be bad for the enviroment.

3. Social networking is common nowdays.

4. Many resturants have to provide lower-cost meals in order to compete.

5. The Internet allows anybody to publish their own writting.

6. The increase in the use of mobile phones has changed the way we do busines.

7. They can take steps to prevent most social and medical problems from occuring.

8. This acid rain can damage plants and animals in the country side.

9. Job satisfaction is indeed very important for the wellbeing of a person.

10. Is it wise to allow employees to wear causal clothes?

11. The numbers for video rentals in the United States were the highest of all figures through out the six-year period.

12. Motorways often go though beautiful areas and may damage plants and wild life.

13. As a result, the earth's tempiture is beginning to rise.

14. I beleive the family is one of the most important structures in sociaty.

15. Goverments should provide money to artists of traditional music and art to maintain the strong tradition of the countris.

Exercise 3　改正下列句子中的大小写错误。

1. the panda of china is an endangered species which has been successfully bred in zoos.

2. these customs are common in muslim countries such as saudi arabia.

3. she started to work for apple in may 2023.

4. i went to university in geneva in switzerland.

5. they took a taxi from york railway station to the royal york hotel in the city centre.

6. however, i do not believe that we generally work longer hours than previously.

7. it is hard to disagree with the suggestion that going to a better school gives a child a better chance at getting admitted to a better University.

8. Americans do not take a long time for meals; they eat and drink for 1.5 Hours each day.

9. during Spring, people all over europe are in gardens and Parks watching wildlife and taking notes.

10. in january, the number of tourists was around One Thousand for the Month, and then increased slightly throughout february.

（答案见 pp. 112~113）

第 2 节　标点使用错误

一　逗号（comma）

逗号是英文中最常用、用法最复杂的标点符号，因此也是写作中最容易出错的标点符号。

1. 要用逗号的情况

（1）起引导介绍作用或连接上下文逻辑的单词、短语、从句后要用逗号

例1　**However,** there are also negative effects of globalisation.

译1　然而，全球化也带来了负面影响。

例2　**On the other hand,** social networking can make it easier to stay in touch with friends.

译2　另一方面，网络社交可以让你更容易地与朋友保持联系。

例3　**Since its invention,** the Internet has changed the way people communicate.

译3　自发明后，互联网改变了人们交流的方式。

例4　**Although I don't like texting,** I like mobile phones.

译4　虽然我不喜欢发短信，但我喜欢手机。

析4　状语从句在前，主句在后，那么状语从句后要加上逗号。

（2）并列结构中要用逗号

例1　Television presents the culture, discoveries, **and** entertainment of foreign countries.

译1　电视呈现外国的文化、新发现和娱乐节目。

例2　Nurses are never listed among the best-paid professionals, **yet** they are more important to our well-being than the movie stars.

译2　护士从来不在收入最高的职业人员之列，但比起电影明星，他们对我们的健康更重要。

析2　由并列连词连接的并列句，并列连词前要用逗号。

（3）句子中间的插入语前后要用逗号

例1　I think, **therefore,** that governments need to raise this awareness in the general public.

译1　因此，我认为政府需要提高公众在这方面的意识。

例2　AI, **on the other hand,** is still fairly new and unfamiliar to most people.

译2　另一方面，人工智能对大多数人来说仍然是相当新奇和陌生的。

例3　My grandmother, **who lives on her own,** is always so pleased to see me.

译3　我祖母一个人住，她每次见到我都很高兴。

析3　出现在句子中间的非限制性定语从句，其前后也要用逗号。

2. 不能用逗号的情况

（1）逗号不能单独连接两个独立分句

两个独立分句之间用逗号连接时需要加上连词，或者改逗号为分号，也可以改用句号分隔为两个句子。

例 His chest heaved, he took a deep breath. ✗

His chest heaved, **and** he took a deep breath. ✓

His chest heaved; he took a deep breath. ✓

His chest heaved. He took a deep breath. ✓

译 他的胸膛上下起伏，然后他深深地吸了一口气。

（2）that从句前、than前不用逗号

例1 Many people believe, **that** strong tradition helps to civilise a nation. ✗

Many people believe **that** strong tradition helps to civilise a nation. ✓

译1 许多人相信，强大的传统有助于使一个国家变得文明。

例2 Fast food restaurants provide take-away meals, **that** can be consumed on the run. ✗

Fast food restaurants provide take-away meals **that** can be consumed on the run. ✓

译2 快餐店提供外卖，让顾客可以在路上吃。

例3 Hardcover books are more expensive, **than** paperback books. ✗

Hardcover books are more expensive **than** paperback books. ✓

译3 精装书比平装书贵。

（3）such as、including短语前有时不加逗号

such as、including后举例的内容若是句子必要成分（限制性的），前面不需要加逗号。反之，则要加逗号。请对比以下两个例句：

例1 Items **such as** mobile phones and computers have become increasingly necessary for business and communication.

译1 手机和计算机等物品在商业和通信中变得越来越必不可少。

例2 People who use computers at work can develop health problems, **such as** wrist problems or back pain.

译2 在工作中使用计算机的人可能会出现健康问题，如手腕问题或背痛。

析 例1中，such as短语修饰的是Items "事物"，这是一个比较宽泛的名词。若删去举例的内容，则句子意思不明确，因此such as短语是必要成分，是限制性的，such as前无须加逗号。例2中，such as短语修饰的是health problems，该短语本身语义具体，举例的内容删去后句子意思也是完整明确的，因此such as短语是非必要成分，是非限制性的，故such as前有逗号。

二 分号（semi-colon）

英文中分号(;)主要用在以下两种情况：一是连接语义紧密的独立分句；二是当并列的语句内部已有逗号，就用分号来分隔这些并列的语句。

例1 Younger school-aged children read stories on smartphones; older kids don't read at all, but hunch over video games.

译1 年龄较小的学龄儿童在智能手机上阅读故事；年龄较大的孩子根本不读书，而是驼着背玩电子游戏。

析1 分号连接两个完整的分句，构成并列句。注意此处分号不能用逗号代替。

例2 The news may be unexpected; **nevertheless**, it is true.

译2 这消息可能出乎意料；然而它是真的。

析2 分号也可以与连接副词一起使用。

例3 My research depicts how the present reading brain enables the development of our intellectual and affective processes: internalized knowledge, analogical reasoning, and inference; perspective-taking and empathy; critical analysis and the generation of insight.

译3 我的研究描述了当前具有阅读能力的大脑如何使我们的智力和情感进程得到发展，这些进程包括：知识的内化、类比思维与推理；观点采择与共情；批判性分析和洞察力的产生。

三　冒号（colon）

英文冒号(:)一般用在列举的内容或同位语之前。

例1 The table illustrates the population of Mexico City, Shanghai, Tokyo and New York in five different years: 1970, 1980, 1990, 2000, and 2001.

译1 该表显示了墨西哥城、上海、东京和纽约四个城市在五个不同年份的人口，包括 1970 年、1980 年、1990 年、2000 年和 2001 年。

析1 冒号后为列举的年份。

例2 I found that learning Italian was useful in the acquisition of more vocabulary in my native language: Spanish.

译2 我发现学习意大利语有助于我积累更多我的母语——西班牙语的词汇。

析2 冒号后为 my native language 的同位语。

Tips

　1. 冒号要用在完整的独立分句之后，be 动词和表语之间不能用冒号（除非加上 the following 或 as follows）。

例 With this in mind, we looked for stocks whose price-to-sales ratios **are:** less than 1, down at least 25% from their five-year averages, and below their ten-year averages. ✗

With this in mind, we looked for stocks whose price-to-sales ratios **are** less than 1, down at least 25% from their five-year averages, and below their ten-year averages. √

With this in mind, we looked for stocks whose price-to-sales ratios **are as follows:** less than 1, down at least 25% from their five-year averages, and below their ten-year averages. √

译 考虑到这一点，我们寻找市销率低于 1，比五年平均水平下降至少 25%，并且低于十年平均水平的股票。

2. such as、for example 后不用冒号。

⑩ People should pay to drive into cities during busy times **such as:** mornings and evenings. ✗

People should pay to drive into cities during busy times **such as** mornings and evenings. √

⑫ 要在繁忙时段，如早上和傍晚，驾车进入市区，应付费。

四 误用中文标点符号

英文标点符号中没有中文中的书名号(《 》)和顿号(、)。书名号在英文用斜体来替代(如果是笔试，由于手写体本身就是斜体，所以其实不必特别标注)，而顿号则用英文的逗号来替代。

此外，中英文的省略号写法有区别，英文省略号是居下的三个点(...)，而中文省略号则是居中的六点(……)，要注意区分。

⑩ My favourite book is《Pride and Prejudice》. ✗

My favourite book is *Pride and Prejudice.* √

⑫ 我最喜欢的书是《傲慢与偏见》。

Exercise 1 在下列句子的必要处加上逗号。若不需要加，则用 C 标记。

1. Overall I believe the advantages are stronger than the disadvantages.

2. After some time it will fly away to begin its adult life and start the cycle again.

3. Traditional medicines are believed by doctors to be healthier and more effective than modern medicines.

4. Because of industrialisation and global trade many traditions have disappeared.

5. However there are certainly dangers in taking time off at that important age.

6. However careful you are accidents can always happen.

7. The graph illustrates changes in the amounts of beef lamb chicken and fish consumed between 1999 and 2023.

8. Some people refuse to go to the zoo because of pity for creatures that must live in small cages.

9. Firstly a person needs to feel that they are doing valued and valuable work so positive feedback from superiors is very important in this respect.

10. More and more people including young children are seriously overweight.

11. I agree that a government should fund its citizens' cultural pursuits.

12. In the UK for example there is currently a shortage of plumbers.

13. Skilled workers are needed for sectors such as information technology and engineering.

14. Use of water per head of population has also increased as people all over the world use more water-consuming items such as washing machines and flush toilets.

15. Fast food is frequently high in fat and salt which when consumed on a regular basis can contribute to health problems like obesity and high blood pressure.

Exercise 2 改正下列句子中的标点符号错误。若没有错误，则用 C 标记。

1. As a result of globalisation the world's cultures are becoming less diverse, people are adopting the customs of countries with strong economies.

2. Expected growth in luxury sales for other regions is: Middle East (8.75%), North America (6%), Europe (3.75%), and Japan (1.75%).

3. Some people argue that happiness can be found in other aspects of life such as: work、family or hobbies.

4. There are many reasons for this, some people blame the amount of junk food that is available, and others claim, it is, because, children don't get enough exercise.

5. The song 《Peace, Love and Happiness》 is dedicated to the children he met there.

6. There are two main types of training; behavioural and obedience.

7. It is important, to make sure that, other people know they cannot pet him, or reward him, if he jumps up.

8. Physical activity could be encouraged relatively cheaply, for example, by installing exercise equipment in parks, as my local council has done.

9. Colour blindness as a matter of fact is more common among men than women.

10. Leeds University which was founded in 1904, has an excellent reputation.

（答案见 pp. 113~114）

第 3 节 名词错误

雅思写作中，最常见的名词错误是对名词的数的错误判断，这涉及一个很重要的语法点——可数名词与不可数名词。

一 可数名词与不可数名词

表示可数的事物的名词，叫作"可数名词"（countable noun），在字典中用 C 表示；表示不可数的事物的名词，叫作"不可数名词"（uncountable noun），在字典中用 U 表示。区分一个名词是可数还是不可数非常重要，这不仅涉及名词本身的单复数变化，还关系到主谓一致的判断以及限定词的选用，甚至会影响到句子的表意准确性（因为有些名词既能用作可数名词又能用作不可数名词，但词义相应会有所变化）。

例1 She has got 15 years' **experience** in the kitchen.

译1 她有 15 年的厨房经验。

析1 表示"经验"时，experience 为不可数名词。

例2 If young people spend too much time online, they may lose valuable social **experiences** that help them develop into confident adults.

译2 如果年轻人花太多时间上网，他们可能会失去宝贵的社交经历，而这些经历有助于他们成长为自信的成年人。

析2 表示"体验，经历"时，experience 为可数名词。此处泛指很多人本应拥有的社交经历，故 experience 要用复数形式，词尾加 -s。

二 常见的可数名词和不可数名词错误

1. 误以为是可数名词的不可数名词

以下是常见的易混淆的不可数名词：

advice 建议	aid 援助，帮助	attention 注意，专心
behaviour 行为	countryside 农村	damage 破坏，损坏
dirt 灰尘，尘土	education 教育	employment 雇用，就业
equipment 设备	furniture 家具	garbage 垃圾
help 帮助	homework 作业	information 信息
knowledge 知识	pollution 污染	research 研究
rubbish 垃圾	software 软件	spending 花费
traffic 交通	transport 交通运输系统	

以 -ing 结尾，描述一项活动的名词均为不可数名词，如：

advertising 做广告	bidding 出价	farming 务农
fishing 钓鱼	marketing 营销	selling 推销
shopping 购物	swimming 游泳	training 训练

2. 因一词多义而产生的混淆

work——表"作品"时可数，表"工作"时不可数

experience——表"经历"时可数，表"经验"时不可数

fortune——表"命运"和"财产"时可数，表"运气"时不可数

time——表"次数"时可数，表"时间"时不可数

glass——表"玻璃杯"时可数，表"玻璃"时不可数

3. 因抽象名词转化为具体名词而产生的混淆

抽象名词通常是不可数的，但是，当它转化为具体名词时，为可数名词。

抽象名词 (不可数)	success 成功	pleasure 愉快	beauty 美，美丽	bother 麻烦
具体名词 (可数)	a success 成功的人或事	a pleasure 令人愉快的人或事	a beauty 美人	a bother 难对付的人或麻烦事

Tips

一些特殊的复数形式

1. stomach 的复数直接加 -s，为 stomachs，而非 stomaches。

2. 以"元音字母 +o"结尾的可数名词从单数变成复数时，直接在其后加 -s，如 radio 的复数形式是 radios。

3. 部分可数单词从单数变成复数时，单词拼写会发生变化，在写作时尤其要注意，如：

单数	复数	释义
bacterium	bacteria	细菌
curriculum	curricula	课程
phenomenon	phenomena	现象

4. 要表示不可数名词的数量，需要在前面加数量单位词。

bread	**a loaf of** bread 一条面包	**two loaves of** bread 两条面包
advice	**a piece of** advice 一条建议	**two pieces of** advice 两条建议
news	**a piece of** news 一则新闻	**two pieces of** news 两则新闻
equipment	**a set of** equipment 一套设备	**two sets of** equipment 两套设备
information	**an item of** information 一则情报	**two items of** information 两则情报
ink	**a bottle of** ink 一瓶墨水	**two bottles of** ink 两瓶墨水

Exercise 1 根据下列单词的意思，注明单词是可数名词（C）还是不可数名词（U）。

1. civilisation _____ 文明   2. performance _____ 表演，演出

3. organisation _____ 组织   4. inspiration _____ 灵感

5. compensation _____ 赔偿金   6. anniversary _____ 周年纪念日

7. mechanism _____ 机制   8. knowledge _____ 知识

9. bilingual _____ 会说两种语言的人 10. conversation _____ 对话，交谈

11. disease _____ 疾病   12. pollution _____ 污染

13. memory _____ 记忆，回忆 14. homework _____ 作业

15. sound _____ 声音   16. behaviour _____ 行为

17. environment _____ 生活环境 18. milk _____ 牛奶

19. variation _____ 变种，变体 20. diversity _____ 多样性

Exercise 2 改正下列句子中名词的使用错误。若没有错误，则用 C 标记。

1. Some environmental damages are permanent.

2. Companies should not be able to make a profit from water.

3. There is a danger of nuclear weapons being obtained by terrorists.

4. Traffic problems in cities increase journey times to work and school.

5. If the focus of university education were learning for pleasures, then students would be happier.

6. With such knowledges of recycling transmitted, the general public will learn and have better insight into it.

7. People should be wary of this new phenomena and not allow it to curb face to face interaction.

8. While there are some benefits to studying independently, I believe group works is usually more productive.

9. The table provides informations about speed and distance for men and women in different major running events.

10. Members of the support network can encourage one another, share personal stories, and offer advices in times of need.

用括号内名词的正确形式填空。

1. Some people believe that charity _____ (organisation) should give aid to those in greatest need, wherever they live.

2. People are shaped by their _____ (experience) of what they see, hear and feel.

3. Animals are used in important scientific _____ (research).

4. Ancient buildings, temples and monuments struggle to cope with a vast amount of visitor _____ (traffic) and get damaged.

5. The most popular subjects for female students were less technical subjects such as social sciences, languages, _____ (literature) and humanities.

6. It is clear that urgent action needs to be taken, since traffic congestion leads to pollution and _____ (frustration).

7. We can deliver _____ (aid) to areas affected by drought, famine and disease much faster, saving many lives.

8. Finally, the planned building work will also include the installation of some kitchen _____ (furniture).

9. It is therefore agreed that technology is a very worthwhile tool for _____ (education).

10. Relatively few students chose destinations other than _____ (employment) and further study.

（答案见 pp. 114~116）

第4节 限定词错误

限定词用于名词短语中，是对中心词进行限定的词类，包括冠词、数词、量词、形容词性物主代词等等。限定词虽小，但是在雅思写作当中却是一个容易出错的语法点。掌握限定词的正确用法，能够保证我们写作的语言准确性，减少失分。

一 正确使用冠词

1. 使用 the 的情况

特指前文提到的人或物或确定的具体对象	例1 He had an excellent idea. **The idea** is to post **the** list on **the** web. 译1 他有一个好主意,就是将名单发布在网上。 例2 **The university** is holding **the** seminar next Monday. 译2 这所大学将在下星期一举行研讨会。 析2 这句话的语境预设读者已知是哪所university和什么seminar。
用在世上独一无二的事物前	**the** world 世界　　　　　　　　**the** Internet 互联网
单数名词前,指代一群(类)人或物	例 I believe that making art classes as a compulsory subject of **the** high school curriculum is necessary. 译 我相信将艺术课设为高中必修课是有必要的。
与最高级或有最高级含义的形容词连用	例1 **The** most surprising result was also **the** most significant. 译1 最令人惊讶的结果也是最有意义的。 例2 We did not know what would happen until **the** final moment. 译2 直到最后一刻我们才知道会发生什么。
与序数词连用	**the** first difficulty 第一个困难
用在由岛屿或州组成的国家或地区名前	**the** United States 美国　　　　　**the** Middle East 中东 **the** UK 英国 (注:其他大部分国家名前不用the,如America、England、China)
用在描述形势、质量或变化等的抽象名词前,这些名词后常跟 of sth.	例1 This advance was brought about by **the development of** antibiotics. 译1 这一进步是由抗生素的发展带来的。 例2 He made a number of recommendations for **the improvement of** staff training. 译2 他就改进人员培训提出了若干建议。 例3 There is a problem with **the availability of** clean water in some villages. 译3 在一些村庄,干净水的供应存在问题。 例4 **The distribution of** income is uneven in most countries. 译4 大多数国家的收入分配不均。

2. 使用 a/an 的情况

用在泛指的或第一次提到的单数可数名词前	例 At the northeastern corner of the town lies **a** shopping mall. 译 城镇的东北角有个购物中心。
表示one这个数量	例 The flat has **a** sitting room and two bedrooms. 译 这套公寓有一个客厅和两个卧室。
表示某一种类和类别	例1 It is **a** beautiful country. 译1 这是一个美丽的国家。 例2 It is **an** international organisation. 译2 这是一个国际组织。
用在职业前	例 She is **a** politician. 译 她是一位政治家。
用在一些常见的名词短语中	to **a** certain extent/degree 在一定程度上 **a** wide range/variety of 多种 **a(n)** large/small/equal number of 大量/少量/相等数量 **a** long time 很长时间

3. 不使用冠词的情况

表示泛指的不可数名词和可数名词复数前	例1 **Behaviour** is much influenced by **colour**. 译1 人的行为在很大程度上受到颜色的影响。 例2 **People** generally react unconsciously to **colour**. 译2 人们对颜色的反应通常是无意识的。
在表示场所的单数名词前,意指其功能	at/in **church** 在做礼拜 at **school** 在上学 in/out of **prison** 坐牢/出狱 in **hospital** 住院
月份、星期前	in **June** 在6月份 on **Monday** 在周一
沟通方式或交通方式前(与**by**搭配)	by **post/email/phone** 以写信/电子邮件/电话的方式 by **car/bus/air/sea** 乘汽车/巴士/飞机/船

 二 常见的限定词错误

	冠词用错的情况
冠词误用	例 Activities are **a** key driver of visitor satisfaction, contributing 74% to visitor satisfaction, while transport and accommodation account for the remaining 26%. 译 活动是提高游客满意度的关键因素,占比为74%,而交通和住宿占剩下的26%。 析 此处a属于冠词误用,a表泛指,the表特指。此处的key driver是特指,故应将a改为the。

冠词冗余	例 It could be argued that New Zealand is **no a** typical destination.
	译 可以说，新西兰不是一个典型的目的地。
	析 no和a都属于中位限定词，不能同时使用，而且意义有重合，no本身就相当于not a，有"不是，并不"的意思，因此应删去a或者把no改为not。

数量词用错的情况	
数量词混淆	例 The waves of electronic equipment could cause **many** damage to our brains.
	译 电子设备的电波可能会对我们的大脑造成许多伤害。
	析 damage表示"伤害，破坏"时是不可数名词，而many修饰可数名词。此处应将many改成plenty of、a lot of等可以修饰不可数名词的数量词。

形容词性物主代词用错的情况	
遗漏形容词性物主代词	例 Many people think that children should be free to enjoy **childhood**.
	译 许多人认为孩子们应该自由自在地享受童年。
	析 此处的childhood指的是children各自的童年，而不是别人的童年，因此childhood前需要加上一个形容词性物主代词明示这一点。与children相对应的形容词性物主代词用their。

Tips

限定词的顺序

限定词可根据其在名词前的搭配位置分为前位、中位和后位限定词。若一个名词短语同时带有这三类限定词，则它们需要按照"前位——中位——后位"的顺序进行排列。另外，要注意一个名词短语前不可同时带有两个前位限定词或两个中位限定词。

- 前位限定词包括：all、both、half；double、twice、two times；one-third、two-thirds；what、such (a/an) 等。
- 中位限定词包括：the、a(n)、this、that、these、those；my、your；John's、the old man's；some、any、no、every、each、either、neither、enough；what(ever)、which(ever)、whose 等。
- 后位限定词包括：one、two；first、second；next、last、(an)other；many、much、(a) few、(a) little、fewer、less、more、most；several、such；plenty of、a lot of、a great number of 等。

例1 And think of **all the other** problems retirement at 55 would create.

译1 想想55岁退休会带来的所有其他问题。

析1 all 为前位限定词，the other 为后位限定词，因此在修饰 problems 时，顺序为 all the other。

例2 Nowadays, many young people in workforce change their jobs or careers **every few** years.

译2 如今，许多已就业的年轻人每隔几年就会换一次工作或职业方向。

析2 every 属于中位限定词，few 为后位限定词，在修饰 years 时，顺序为 every few。

Exercise 1 选词填空。

1. _____ (Many/Much) fathers and mothers share their parenting and domestic responsibilities.
2. Subsidising artists helps them fully develop _____ (their/they) potential and benefits the public as well.
3. We have studied only 5 per cent of _____ (the/不用冠词) species we know.
4. Some people say it is beneficial to teaching and learning because there is so _____ (many/much) information available.
5. It allows you to store _____ (all your/your all) Internet passwords.

Exercise 2 改正下列句子中的冠词错误。

1. Education is key to a successful career.
2. Poverty is major issue in many developing countries.
3. The pollution is a serious problem in the many cities.
4. A people should be able to express their opinions freely.
5. Education is important for the children to succeed in the life.
6. The government should provide a free healthcare to all citizens.
7. The government needs to invest in the renewable energy sources.
8. The culture of country is shaped by its the history and traditions.
9. The technology has changed the way we communicate with the others.
10. The social media has become a popular way to connect with the friends.

（答案见 p. 116）

第 5 节　动词错误

　　动词是英文句子的关键成分，而其变化与用法较为繁杂，因此也是写作过程中的易错点。本节以谓语动词为重点，从主谓一致、时态、与非谓语动词的搭配三个角度讲解雅思写作中应该如何正确使用动词。

一　主谓一致

　　主谓一致的含义是：谓语动词在人称和数上要与主语保持一致。以下是常见的规律。

1. 用单数动词的情况

（1）主语为单数名词

例 First, *every single person* **needs** food each day and **has** a right to it.

译 首先，每个人每天都需要食物，并且有权利得到食物。

（2）主语为不可数名词

例 Admittedly, *gender inequality* **was** a highly controversial issue in the twentieth century.

译 诚然，性别不平等在二十世纪是一个极具争议的问题。

（3）主语为动名词（doing）

例 *Banning* private cars **reduces** traffic jam.

译 禁止私家车可以减缓交通拥堵。

（4）主语为What引导的从句

例 *What we can do* **is** use the media responsibly and not let it use us.

译 我们能做的是负责任地使用媒体，而不是让它利用我们。

（5）主语为不定代词each

例 *Each* of these stages **takes place** in a very different aquatic location.

译 每个阶段都发生在不同的水域。

（6）主语为the number/percentage/proportion of等与名词构成的名词短语

例 In 1971, *the number of* households in owned accommodation **was** higher than last year.

译 1971年，自有住房的家庭数量比起上一年有所增长。

2. 用复数动词的情况

（1）主语为复数名词

例 *Coconut palms* **produce** as many as seventy fruits per year, weighing more than a kilogram each.

译 椰子树每年生产的果实多达70颗，每颗重超过1公斤。

（2）主语为some、several、both、few、many、a number of、a majority/minority of后接复数名词

例1 *A number of jobs* **have been lost** as a direct result of new computer technology.

译1 新的计算机技术直接导致许多工作岗位流失。

例2 There **are** *several alternatives* to guns.

译2 枪支有几种替代品。

（3）由and连接两个或两个以上主语时（这些主语分别指不同的人或物）

例 A rise in global temperature *and* a fall in human fitness level **are** often **viewed** as being caused by the expanding use of automobiles.

译 全球气温上升和人类健康水平下降通常被认为是汽车使用量增加导致的。

3. 特殊情况

（1）主语带有a lot of、most of、any of、half of、ninety percent of、none of、the rest of、all of、plenty of等限定词

　　这些限定词后接不可数名词或单数名词作主语时，谓语动词用单数。

例1 Just over *half of the radiation* **is absorbed** by the Earth.

译1 正好一多半的辐射被地球吸收。

　　这些限定词后接复数名词作主语时，谓语动词用复数。

例2 *Most of the people* who attend the classes **find** it is a nice way of getting to know one another.

译2 大多数参加这些课程的人都发现这是一种互相了解的好方法。

例3 Practically *all of the creature comforts* that we now take for granted **were made** possible by modern communication technology.

译3 几乎所有我们现在认为理所当然的物质享受都是现代通信科技带来的。

（2）就近原则

　　有时谓语动词的人称和数与离它最近的主语保持一致。比如，由either... or、neither... nor、not only... but also连接两个名词或代词作并列主语时，谓语动词应与后一个主语的人称和数一致；There be句型的be动词的数也由离be最近的主语决定。

例 Neither your tutor nor *your parents* **guarantee** your continuous improvement.

译 你的导师和父母都不能保证你持续进步。

（3）主语是由and连接的多个名词，而这些名词指同一人或物

　　由and连接两个或两个以上名词作主语时，如这些名词指同一人或物，其后谓语动词用单数。

例 *The singer and dancer* **takes part in** the race.

译 那位歌舞演员参加了比赛。

析 dancer前没有定冠词the，因此singer和dancer是指同一人的多个身份，故谓语动词用第三人称单数形式takes part in。

（4）主语是"the+形容词/过去分词"短语

　　"the+形容词/过去分词"作主语，表示一类人时，谓语动词用复数形式；如果指个别人或表示抽象概念，谓语动词要用单数形式。

例1 *The elderly* probably **do not accept** modern communication technology as other age groups do.

译1 老年人对现代通信科技的接受程度可能不如其他年龄段的人。

例2 *The new* **is** to replace the old.

译2 新事物终将取代旧事物。

（5）集合名词

　　集合名词强调整体概念时，谓语动词用单数形式；如果是强调其中的个体，谓语动词则用复数形式。

例1 The traditional structure of men working and women staying at home means that *the family* **has** more economic benefits.

译1 "男主外，女主内"的传统架构意味着家庭能获得更多经济效益。

析1 family在这个句子中指"整个家庭"，应视作单数，故谓语动词也用单数形式。

例2 *The family* **live** in a simple, single-storey house.

译2 这家人住在一栋简单的单层房屋里。

析2 family在这个句子中强调"家里的每个人"，为复数含义，故谓语动词用复数形式。

二 谓语动词的时态

　　在雅思写作中，特别是小作文，要注意时态的选用。

　　概述图表用一般现在时，如The graph shows... "图表显示……"或We can see... "我们可以看到……"。

　　在描述具体数值和趋势变化时，均应根据其所对应的具体时间来确定时态。也就是说，介绍过去时间的数据或趋势用一般过去时；介绍将来的数据预测则应该用一般将来时，或用be expected/predicted to的结构；如句子时间状语为"since+时间点"或"by+时间点"，则应用完成时态。

例1 The graph **shows** the popularity of three different types of holiday from 1990 to 2020 in millions of travellers.

译1 该图显示了1990年至2020年三种不同类型的度假形式在数百万游客中的受欢迎程度。

例2 From 2010 to 2020, there **was** a sharp drop in the number of people who went on skiing holidays.

译2 从2010年到2020年，滑雪度假的人数急剧下降。

例3 The number of job vacancies **is predicted to** continue to rise and reach 30,000 by 2030.

译3 职位空缺数量预计将继续上升，到2030年将达到30,000个。

例4 Land used for housing **has decreased** since 1980.

译4 自1980年以来，住房用地有所减少。

例5 By 2015, expenditure on food and drink **had fallen** by 4% in New Zealand.

译5 到2015年，新西兰的食品和饮料支出下降了4%。

除了并列谓语的情况，一个简单句只能有一个谓语动词，绝对不允许两个谓语动词同时存在。如果一个简单句中除了谓语动词之外还需要用到其他动词，那么其他动词就要采用非谓语动词形式。非谓语动词有三种形式——to do(不定式)、doing(动名词或现在分词)和done(过去分词)，它们可以充当主语、宾语、定语、状语等成分。

　　其中最常见的一个用法是to do和doing跟在谓语动词后作其宾语。至于是用to do还是用doing，很多同学常常分不清。以下列出雅思写作中一些常用到的固定搭配。

1. "动词 +doing" 的常用搭配

practice doing sth. 练习做某事

prohibit doing sth. 禁止做某事

suggest doing sth. 建议做某事

resist doing sth. 抗拒做某事

finish doing sth. 完成做某事

imagine doing sth. 想象做某事

consider doing sth. 考虑做某事

mind doing sth. 介意做某事

avoid doing sth. 避免做某事

admit doing sth. 承认做某事

deny doing sth. 否认做某事

escape doing sth. 逃避做某事

give up doing sth. 放弃做某事

keep doing sth. 保持做某事

enjoy doing sth. 享受做某事

be/get used to doing sth. 习惯于做某事

2. "动词 +to do" 的常用搭配

agree to do sth. 同意做某事

offer to do sth. 主动提出做某事

manage to do sth. 设法做某事

arrange to do sth. 安排做某事

refuse to do sth. 拒绝做某事

aim to do sth. 打算做某事

hope to do sth. 希望做某事

pretend to do sth. 假装做某事

choose to do sth. 选择做某事

decide to do sth. 决定做某事

afford to do sth. 负担得起做某事

expect to do sth. 期待做某事

plan to do sth. 计划做某事

fail to do sth. 未能做某事

promise to do sth. 承诺做某事

wish to do sth. 想要做某事

attempt to do sth. 试图做某事

3. "动词 +doing/to do" 意思相同的搭配

prefer to do/doing sth. 更喜欢做某事

continue to do/doing sth. 继续做某事

start to do/doing sth. 开始做某事

intend to do/doing sth. 想要做某事

cease to do/doing sth. 停止做某事

begin to do/doing sth. 开始做某事

love to do/doing sth. 喜爱做某事

hate to do/doing sth. 憎恨做某事

4. "动词 +doing/to do" 意思不同的搭配

　　有的动词后面既可以加doing也可以加to do，但是意思不一样。若在雅思写作中将两者混淆，容易造成语义上的错误。

stop doing sth. 停止做(正在做的)某事

go on doing sth. 继续做(一直在做的)某事

forget doing sth. 忘记做过某事(动作已发生)

remember doing sth. 记得做过某事(动作已发生)

regret doing sth. 后悔做了某事(动作已发生)

try doing sth. 尝试做某事

stop to do sth. 停下(手头的事)去做(另外的)某事

go on to do sth. (做完一件事后)接着做(另外的)某事

forget to do sth. 忘记去做某事(动作未发生)

remember to do sth. 记得去做某事(动作未发生)

regret to do sth. 对将要做某事感到抱歉(动作未发生)

try to do sth. 努力做某事

要掌握动词后是接 to do 还是 doing，关键在于注重积累和记忆其搭配用法。除此之外，我们也可以通过了解两个基本的语法本质帮助我们进一步区分，从而减轻部分记忆负担，即：

①不定式由助动词变化而来，带有不确定的语气。

②动名词的结构接近普通名词，往往带有"动作持续"的意味。

例1 The government **plans to change** their policy on air travel.

译1 政府计划改变其航空旅行政策。

析1 plans 后面用不定式 to change 是因为这一动作是打算做但还没做的事，相当于 The government is going to change...，是发生在将来的动作，具有不确定性。同样，promise、hope、expect 等有不确定性含义的动词后面也要接不定式。

例2 Finally, **avoid signing** any business contract before you have read and understood it thoroughly.

译2 最后，在你没有通读和完全理解的情况下，不要签署任何商业合同。

析2 avoid "避免"具有否定意义，需要避免的是 sign "签署"这一行为，这一行为是确定的，已经发生过或正在发生，因此才要避免再次出现，故此处用 sign 的 doing 形式。同样用法的还有 admit、practice、enjoy 等词。

理解以上两点，就能很好区分 remember/forget/stop to do sth. 和 remember/forget/stop doing sth. 的区别了。

例3 **Remember to pull** the laces firmly when you put these boots on as they are rather wide around the ankles.

译3 穿这双靴子时，记得要用力拉紧鞋带，因为靴子的脚踝处比较宽。

析3 "记得要……拉紧鞋带"的"拉紧鞋带"这个动作未发生，具有不确定性，所以用不定式 to pull。

例4 I **remember pulling** the laces firmly when I put these boots on.

译4 我记得我穿上这双靴子时鞋带系得很紧。

析4 "记得……鞋带系得很紧"的"鞋带系得很紧"是已经发生的事情，没有不确定性，而且可以理解为是从过去一直持续的状态，所以用动名词 pulling。

小试牛刀

Exercise 1 判断下列句子主语的单复数，用括号内单词的正确形式填空。

1. There _____ (be) plenty of evidence to suggest that children are overweight, and the situation is getting worse.

2. I think that it is wise to take an intermediate position because each of these ways _____ (have) its own advantages.

3. The young in particular _____ (be) willing to accept this concept.

4. But what began as nothing important in public affairs _____ (have) grown into a social movement.

5. Hollywood's theory that machines with evil minds _____ (drive) armies of killer robots is just silly.

6. The number of graduates participating in each activity _____ (be) higher than that of postgraduates.

7. Moreover, both mothers and fathers _____ (be) becoming aware of the freedom to choose the role they will have in the upbringing of their children.

8. It is the public that _____ (have) the power to make such destructive policies unprofitable and illegal.

9. Very few children _____ (go) to school, particularly not poor children so they learn in other ways.

10. If there _____ (be) access to a reliable source of water, there _____ (be) great potential for the development of agriculture.

Exercise 2 判断下列句子的时态，用括号内单词的正确形式填空。

1. There _____ (be) a slight increase in holidays to France between 2006 and 2007.

2. From 2020 to 2040 it is predicted that there _____ (be) a sharp rise in the number of people who go on skiing holidays.

3. Beach holidays _____ (decrease) gradually from over 4 million to 3.5 million travellers since 2020.

4. The cost of accommodation _____ (go down) gradually for thirty years after 1990.

5. The graph _____ (show) how many tourists _____ (visit) three countries in the summer of 2009.

Exercise 3 根据句意，选择合适的选项。

1. The government is planning _____ a complete smoking ban.

    A. introducing   B. to introduce   C. introduced   D. introduce

2. If everyone decides _____ at least twice a week, this might have a significant effect on levels of pollution.

    A. walking   B. walked   C. to walk   D. walk

3. Unfortunately, many people are unable to resist _____ their cars because they have busy lives.

    A. using   B. use   C. to use   D. used

4. Many people enjoy _____ , but they should try _____ as much as possible.

    A. to drive; to walk   B. to drive; walking

    C. driving; to walk   D. driving; walking

5. I have finished _____ my research, so I need to start _____ my dissertation.

    A. to do; work on   B. to do; working on

    C. doing; to working on   D. doing; working on

Exercise 4 用括号内单词的 doing 或 to do 形式填空。

1. Most years we have a children's choir, but this year the local army cadets offered _____ (perform).

2. What people sometimes don't realise when they start is that it takes a lot of determination and hard work to keep _____ (train) week after week.

3. Nowadays, more and more people decide _____ (have) children later in their life.

4. So, when I began _____ (do) some of the household tasks by myself, I began _____ (respect) the job of others and tried _____ (collect) all my toys after my playing with them.

5. Although attempting _____ (rescue) the world from poverty is an admirable cause, I maintain that charity organisations should focus their efforts on the local population.

（答案见 pp. 116~118）

第6节　介词错误

虽然介词只是虚词，不能单独构成句子成分，但用好介词能大大提升文章的简洁度，令表达更地道。使用介词时要注意遵循固定搭配，并保证"介宾结构"完整，否则就会出现语法错误，或令意思出现偏差。

一　短语搭配错误

在雅思写作中，常见的介词错误之一就是搭配有误，这样的错误会影响作文的流畅性和准确性，最终影响成绩。因此，同学们平时要注意积累，把常见的固定搭配熟记在心，避免出现介词搭配错误。

以下是雅思写作中常用但容易用错介词的固定搭配短语：

as a result of 是……的结果，由于	be distributed to 分发到
be wary of 对……感到警惕	be destined for 注定
be beneficial to 有助于	be deprived of 失去，被剥夺
take responsibility for 为……负责	in response to 对……的回应
resign oneself to 顺从接受	be incapable of 对……无能为力
with respect to 关于	take account of 考虑到
be faced with 面对	at the expense of 以……为代价
associate... with 把……与……联系起来	have effects on 对……有影响

二　介词后的宾语错误

介词后面要接名词、代词或相当于名词的其他词类、短语或从句等，构成"介宾结构"。因此，若介词后面是一个动词，则需要使用doing形式，变成动名词作介词宾语。在雅思写作中，介词后面的动词没有使用doing形式也是高频错误之一。

例1 When we look at a piece of art, we can be moved in ways that science and technology **are incapable of** replicating.

译1 我们欣赏艺术品时会受到触动，这种方式是科技复制不来的。

析1 在这个句子中，be incapable of 意为"对……无能为力"，of 是介词，因此后面的动词 replicate 需要用 doing 形式，即 replicating。

例2 By the time a student reaches the university level, they are required to complete multiple hours of independent study each day **in addition to** attending face-to-face classes.

译2 等到孩子上了大学，除了要参加面对面的课堂学习，每天他们还会被要求完成数小时的自主学习。

析2 在这个句子中，in addition to 意为"除……之外"，其中 to 是介词，因此其后面的动词 attend 用 doing 形式。

> **Tips**
>
> 英语中常见的 to do sth. 是动词不定式的用法，to 后面的动词用原形。但在一些短语中，to 是介词，其后应该跟动词的 doing 形式，同学们需要注意两者的区别。
>
> 雅思写作中常见的 to 作为介词的搭配有：
>
> get used to (doing) sth. 习惯于做某事　　　　commit to (doing) sth. 保证做某事
>
> be devoted to (doing) sth. 献身于做某事　　　owing to (doing) sth. 因为，由于
>
> resign oneself to (doing) sth. 顺从接受做某事

值得强调的是，名词性从句也可以充当介词宾语，正确使用"介词 + 从句"的结构可以丰富写作句型。雅思写作中常见的搭配是 the question/problem/debate of whether...，意为"关于是否……的问题 / 争论"。

例3 The issue **of** whether we should group or segregate students with varying talents and abilities has generated mixed views in recent years.

译3 近年来，在是否要将天资和能力不同的学生分开上课这一问题上，人们存在不同的看法。

析3 在这个句子中，介词 of 后面接的是一个由 whether 引导的宾语从句。

三 正确使用介词描述趋势和变化

在雅思小作文中，常遇到要描述趋势和变化的情况，这时也可以使用介词来表达。主要有以下两种表达，注意不要混淆两种表达所用的介词。

1. 描述某样事物总体的变化趋势

(表示趋势或变化的)名词 +in+ 名词(短语)						
a(n)	+	cut、decline、decrease、drop、reduction；increase、rise、growth、improvement；change、trend、variation	+	in	+	sth.

例1 The chart shows **a decline in** deforestation in the area.
译1 这张图表显示该地区的森林砍伐行为减少了。

例2 Overall, there was **a drop in** the amount of other pollution.
译2 总体来说，其他污染物的排放量在减少。

例3 Changes to the social stigma attached to singleness have led to **a rise in** the number of living alone.
译3 社会对单身的偏见发生了变化，导致了独居人口的增加。

例4 There has been **a change in** the number of students studying Mandarin.
译4 学习普通话的学生人数发生了变化。

2. 描述具体的数值变化

(表示变化或变化结果的)名词 +of+ 数字						
a(n)	+	fall、decrease、drop、reduction；increase、rise；low、high、maximum、peak、total	+	of	+	number

例1 In Year Three, there was **a drop of** £2,000 in room renting.
译1 第三年度，房屋租赁收入下降了 2,000 英镑。

例2 2013 saw **a rise of** one million tourist visits to each country.
译2 2013 年，每个国家的游客访问量都增加了 100 万人次。

例3 Nationally, Canada produced the most uranium—9,476 tonnes, followed by Australia with **a total of** 8,611 tonnes.

译3 各国横向对比，加拿大的铀产量最多，达9,476吨，其次是澳大利亚，总计8,611吨。

四 正确使用介词描述统计数据

在雅思写作中，描述统计数据时常常需要用到介词，如of、between、for、at和with等。以下是各介词的常用搭配。

（1）X% of sth.

例 Spanish-speaking British students made up 30% **of** the total number of British students at the university in 2000.

译 2000年，说西班牙语的英国学生占该大学英国学生总数的30%。

（2）between A and B

例1 The percentage of malnourished elderly people in the EU fell gradually **between** 1970 **and** 1980.

译1 1970年至1980年间，欧盟营养不良老年人的比例逐渐下降。

例2 The charts below show household spending patterns in two countries **between** 1980 **and** 2008.

译2 下图显示了1980年至2008年间两国的家庭支出模式。

（3）the figure for (a group)

例 Although flats rose by 2% to 9% in Tasmania, **the figure for** semi-detached houses in this area stabilised at 4%.

译 尽管塔斯马尼亚州的公寓增加了2%，达到9%，但半独立式房屋的数量仍旧维持在4%。

（4）the percentage of (a group)

例 **The percentage of** 30—39s and 20—29s was similar, representing 16% and 11% respectively.

译 30—39岁和20—29岁的人群比例相似，分别为16%和11%。

（5）at a rate (of X%)

例 Customers who use fitting rooms in order to try on clothes buy the product they are considering **at a rate of** 85%, compared with 58% for those that do not do so.

译 使用试衣间试穿考虑购买的衣服后买下商品的顾客比例为85%，相比之下，不试穿衣服就购买的顾客比例为58%。

（6）be highest/come top/rank first with sth.

例 The United Kingdom **ranked** second **with** an employment rate of approximately 90%.

译 英国以约90%的就业率排名第二。

Exercise 1　在横线上填入适当的介词。

1. Many gifted children are deprived _____ the opportunity to be intellectually challenged.

2. Whether high level education or skills and experience are needed depends _____ the position you apply for.

3. Ultimately, as long as people are willing to support crime prevention initiatives and take responsibility _____ their own personal protection, there will always be ways to help reduce crime.

4. In contrast, many people have resigned themselves _____ the fact that nothing can be done to prevent crime.

5. People who have worked in the same industry for more than 20 years have undoubtedly been faced _____ difficult decisions.

Exercise 2　改正下列句子中的介词搭配错误。

1. Many people, however, are wary about journalists and reluctant to trust their work.

2. In many areas of the world, temperature and climate have adverse effects to public health.

3. The question for whether or not parents should be actively involved in children's literacy is an issue worthy of debate.

4. Being innovative and creative is beneficial at problem-solving skills and prepares students for their future study.

5. In my opinion, one cannot expect to rely on success from money or appearance, and people must dedicate themselves in a life of hard work and resilience, and never give up.

6. Thousands of plant and animal species are now extinct as a direct result from human influence, and the rate of extinction is continuing to increase with each passing year.

7. In order to be adequately prepared for the lifelong task of raising a child, prospective parents should commit to learn the essential skills necessary for becoming a good parent.

8. In addition to developing essential skills to more young people for their future lives and careers and increasing their likelihood of secure a high-paying job, expansion of university widens the pool of skilled candidates for prospective employers.

Exercise 3　用画线部分的名词形式改写句子。

1. The table shows that primary school numbers have <u>fallen</u> by 10%.
   The table shows _____.

2. The government hopes to <u>reduce</u> the number of cars coming into cities.
   The government hopes to achieve _____.

3. Electronic device usage has <u>risen</u> by 30% since the introduction of digital communication technology.
   Since the introduction of digital communication technology, there has been _____
   _____.

4. The number of newly graduated students in Britain <u>peaked</u> at around 195,000 in 1997.
   The number of newly graduated students in Britain reached _____.

5. Some people say the best way to <u>improve</u> public health is by increasing the number of sports facilities.
   Some people say the best way to make _____.

（答案见 pp. 118~119）

第7节　混淆连词和副词

连词，顾名思义就是起连接作用的词，它可以连接单词、短语和句子，表示并列或从属的关系。**副词**则是用来表示行为和状态特征的词，它具有修饰作用，常用以修饰动词、形容词、副词或句子。

在雅思写作中，同学们往往没有正确掌握连词和副词的区别，从而出现这两类词的误用，造成句子出现语法错误，导致写作失分。以下是一些容易混淆的连词和副词，同学们应多加留意。

一　however 作连词和作副词的区别

1. however 作连词

however 作从属连词时，意为"不管怎样，无论如何"，引导让步状语从句。

例 **However** we adopt healthcare reform, it isn't going to save major amounts of money.

译 不管我们采取何种医疗改革措施，都不会节省太多钱。

析 however在此句中为从属连词，引导we adopt healthcare reform这一从句。

2. however 作副词

（1）意为"然而，但是"时，可以放于句首、句中或句末，以逗号隔开

例1 **However,** there is no reason why job satisfaction and job security cannot go hand in hand as long as people enjoy their work first and foremost.

译1 然而，只要以喜欢工作为前提，工作满足感和工作保障没有理由不能兼顾。

例2 In my opinion, **however,** catering to individual preference is secondary to benefiting society as a whole.

译2 但我认为，比起造福全社会，满足个人偏好是次要的。

析 在这两个例句中，however都是作为副词使用，表示转折。若放在句首，应写成"However,"，若放在句中，前后应有逗号隔开，写成"，however,"。

Tips

however 作副词表示"然而，但是"时的常见错误

只有当 however 作为副词且放在句中时，才可写成"，however,"，此时 however 只用于表达转折的意义，去掉后不影响句子结构的完整性。若把表示转折意思的"，however,"放在两个完整的分句之间则是错误的写法，错误地把 however 当作连词去使用，如以下例子所示：

例 The solution to this problem is by no means easy, **however,** there are certain precautions that we can all take to help minimize the harmful effects on the environment.

译 解决这个问题并非易事，但是我们可以采取一定的预防措施，使对环境的不利影响最小化。

析 在这个句子中，however意为"但是"，是一个副词，不是连词，不能以上面这种形式连接两个独立分句，若想用连词来表达"但是"，可以用but，正确的写法是：

The solution to this problem is by no means easy. **However,** there are certain precautions that we can all take to help minimize the harmful effects on the environment. (However是副词)

或 The solution to this problem is by no means easy, **but** there are certain precautions that we can all take to help minimize the harmful effects on the environment. (but是连词)

（2）意为"不管多么，无论到什么程度"时，与副词或形容词连用

例 That is not to suggest everyone should dance their way to work, **however** healthy and happy it might make us.

译 这并不是说每个人都应该在上班的路上跳舞，不管这会让我们多么健康和快乐。

析 在这个句子中，however是副词，修饰形容词healthy和happy。

二 therefore 和 so 的区别

在雅思写作中，therefore和so都是常用的词，表示"因此，所以"，但是取这个义项时，两者词性不同，therefore为副词，而so为连词。试比较以下例句：

例1 **Therefore,** the use of mobile phones in public places should not be banned.

译1 因此，在公共场合使用手机不应该被禁止。

例2 Many people blame excessive violence in television programmes and movies for the increasing rate of violent crimes, **and therefore** government censorship of such media content should be imposed.

译2 许多人把不断上升的暴力犯罪率归咎于电视节目和电影中过多的暴力镜头，因此政府应该对这些媒体的内容进行审查。

例3 Due to the lack of alternative viewing options, it was difficult to judge the relative quality of programmes, **so** complaints of declining standards were rare.

译3 由于缺少可替代的观看选择，很难去判断节目的相对质量，所以鲜有标准下降的投诉。

析 在雅思写作中，therefore作为副词，一般放在句子开头，随后用逗号隔开，如例1。若想要把therefore放在中间连接两个分句，则需要加连词and，因为therefore是副词，不能连接分句，如例2。若想要表达"因此，所以"的意思，又需要连接两个分句，除了像例2用and therefore，还可以单独使用连词so，如例3。切勿出现以下混淆副词和连词用法的错误：

- Many people blame... of violent crimes, **therefore** government censorship of such media content should be imposed. ✗

- Due to the lack of... programmes**, so,** complaints of declining standards were rare. ✗

Tips

在雅思写作中，常见的副词还有besides/moreover/hence/thus/in contrast/in addition等，常用的连词还有and/although/because/since等，要避免在使用它们时出现语法错误，关键在于理解它们在词性上的区别：连词可用于连接两个分句，使之成为一个完整的句子。副词用来表达概念，起修饰的作用，去掉不影响句子的结构，不可连接分句。

小试牛刀

Exercise 1 改正下列句子中的连词或副词使用错误。

1. Bottled water is now a $100 billion business, and, 81 per cent of the bottles are not recycled.

2. Human evolution and technological advancement have helped make the world a better place, but, they have also come at a cost to the environment.

3. The majority of learning used to come from the reading of books, however, the Internet has changed the way we access information and consequently rendered books obsolete.

4. More often than not, criminal behaviour results from social or environmental factors, therefore the argument that criminals are born rather than made is not valid.

5. Transportation is estimated to account for 30% of energy consumption, so, lowering the need for energy-using vehicles is essential for decreasing the environmental impact of mobility.

6. Some people feel that too much emphasis is put on passing exams. Because pupils spend a large proportion of school time doing tests rather than learning.

Exercise 2 选词填空。

1. Government financial support, _____ (however/but), should also be used to maintain the quality of the university since tuition and donation are not constant sources of funding and are not necessarily sufficient.

2. _____ (Moreover/Although) the destruction to school property was considerable, I believe that in this case the punishment fits the crime, and the boy was appropriately diverted away from the prison system.

3. _____ (In contrast/Unless), when we do what we love and love what we do, we are fully motivated and cannot wait to start work each day.

4. The rise of social media has transformed the way we communicate and connect with others. _____ (Moreover/Yet), it has a profound effect on how we view the world.

5. Many countries are implementing measures to reduce carbon emissions and combat climate change. _____ (Therefore/So that), it is essential that individuals also make changes to their daily habits to reduce their carbon footprints.

（答案见 pp. 119~120）

第②章　如何写出正确的句子

第1节　如何扩充简单句

在雅思写作中，基本的简单句是最直接、最容易被理解的句子，适用于表达观点。但基本的简单句能够传达的信息有限，要想在雅思写作中取得高分，需要做到在正确写出简单句的基础上将其扩充和具体化。以下是几种扩充简单句的方式。

一　添加限定词和修饰词

在雅思写作中，通过添加限定词（如冠词、数词、名词所有格等）和修饰词（如形容词和名词等），我们可以对事物进行进一步描述，事物内涵就会更加明确。

例1 Environmental pollution is a cause of preventable illnesses and diseases worldwide.

扩1 Environmental pollution is **one of the biggest** causes of preventable illnesses and diseases worldwide.

译1 环境污染是引起世界各地可预防疾病的最大原因之一。

析1 在原句中，主语是 Environmental pollution，谓语是 is，表语是 a cause of preventable illnesses and diseases。通过添加限定词 one of 和形容词最高级 the biggest 来修饰 causes，其意思更加准确，而且补充说明了环境污染是一个多么重要的原因。

例2 Without will power, a person cannot overcome difficulties while striving for success.

扩2 Without **strong** will power, a person cannot overcome **unavoidable** difficulties while striving for success.

译2 没有坚强的意志力，一个人在奋力追求成功的过程中就无法克服不可避免的困难。

析2 在原句的基础上，添加 strong 和 unavoidable 两个形容词分别修饰 will power 和 difficulties，使得叙述更加有力，突出了坚强意志力的作用。

二　添加介词短语

在雅思写作中，若想补充说明事件发生的时间、地点或方式等或补充描述对象的详细信息，可在简单句的基础上添加介词短语来表达。

例 The bar charts illustrate data.

扩1 The bar charts illustrate data **about the underground rail networks in six cities**.

扩2 The bar charts illustrate data about the underground rail networks in six cities, **in terms of their age, size and annual ridership**.

译 这些柱状图显示了六个城市地下铁路网的数据，包括它们投入使用的时间、规模和年客流量。

析 在原句中，主语是 The bar charts，谓语是 illustrate，宾语是 data，三者构成了"主+谓+宾"结构的简单句。但是，这一简单句的意思并不完整，因此扩1的例句添加了"介词 about+名词短语 the underground rail networks in six cities"的介宾结构来补充说明数据的主题。在此基础上，还可以继续添加 in terms of 介词短语补充具体信息，如扩2中，in terms of their age, size and annual ridership 补充说明了有哪些方面的数据。

三 添加非谓语动词

1. 非谓语动词充当定语

　　非谓语动词作定语,用来修饰名词,常译成"……的"。在雅思写作中,同学们需要注意正确使用非谓语动词 doing、done 和 to do 这三种形式。

例1　In 2004, there were 600 pupils and the two school buildings were separated by a path.

扩1　In 2004, there were 600 pupils **attending the school**, and the two school buildings were separated by a path **running from the main entrance to the sports field**.

译1　2004年,有600名小学生在这所学校上学,两栋教学楼被一条从正门通往操场的小路隔开。

析1　在原句中,there were 600 pupils 是基本的 There be 句型。在扩充句子时,可以添加非谓语动词来进一步描述 pupils 这个主语,例句添加的是 attending the school 作后置定语。因为 pupils 和 attend 是主动关系,因此用了 doing 形式,译为"在这所学校上学的"。而 the two school buildings were separated by a path 则是"主+谓(被动语态)"结构,在扩充句子时,添加非谓语动词短语 running from... field 作 a path 的后置定语,a path 和 run 是主动关系,因而也用 doing 形式,该现在分词短语意为"一条从正门通往操场的"。添加非谓语动词短语对名词进行补充说明后,句子中所描述的对象变得更加明确。

例2　The information remained accurate.

扩2　The information **provided** remained accurate.

译2　所提供的信息仍然准确。

析2　原句是"主+系(remained)+表"的基本结构。当我们想要进一步说明是"什么信息",且此修饰成分与动作相关时,可以使用非谓语动词来充当 information 的定语,如扩充句中,information 是"被提供的",故用过去分词 provided。

例3　Another motive for collecting is the desire.

扩3　Another motive for collecting is the desire **to find something special**.

译3　收集的另一个动机是寻找特别东西的欲望。

析3　原句是"主+系+表"的结构,其中主语 motive 带有一个介词短语 for collecting 作其后置定语。句子意思为"收集的另一个动机是欲望",但没有指出是什么欲望。因此,扩充句加上非谓语动词短语 to find something special 修饰 desire,充当其定语,意为"寻找特别东西的",进一步说明具体是什么欲望促使人们收集东西。

2. 非谓语动词充当状语

　　在雅思写作中,可以添加非谓语动词作状语补充说明事件的时间、目的、原因、结果、条件等。

例　We can see that small huts have been built.

扩　**Looking at the maps in more detail**, we can see that small huts have been built **to accommodate visitors to the island**.

译　仔细看一下地图,我们可以看到岛上建造了小棚屋,来为游客提供住宿。

析　扩充后的句子添加了两个非谓语动词短语作状语。句首的 doing 短语作方式状语,表示 see 的方式,look at 与逻辑主语 we 之间是主动关系,所以用 doing 形式。句末的 to do 短语则用来表示建造小棚屋的目的。加上了方式状语和目的状语后,句子意义明显丰富了很多。

四 添加同位语和插入语

同位语和插入语可以是一个单词、一个短语甚至是一个从句,常伴有一些标志性的标点符号,如逗号、括号、破折号等。在雅思写作中,它们可以用来进一步解释名词或补充说明观点。

例1 The city of Paris is one of the most popular tourist destinations in the world.

扩1 The city of Paris, **the capital of France**, is one of the most popular tourist destinations in the world.

译1 法国首都巴黎是世界上最受欢迎的旅游目的地之一。

析1 本例通过添加主语The city of Paris的同位语the capital of France,补充了"巴黎是法国的首都"这一信息,实现了句子的扩充。

例2 Prices rose sharply for fresh fruits and vegetables.

扩2 Prices, **particularly after 1989**, rose sharply for fresh fruits and vegetables.

译2 特别是在1989年之后,新鲜水果和蔬菜的价格急剧上涨。

析2 扩充后的句子使用了插入语particularly after 1989来补充说明价格上涨的时间节点。

Exercise 1 选词填空。（每个词仅用一次）

made	steep	major	by	one of
to enhance	for	starting	to purify	abrupt

1. Most managers can identify the _____ trends of the day.

2. Global warming, _____ the most serious issues in modern life, also affects people's health and well-being.

3. More young people are moving to cities _____ work opportunities as well as all the facilities and opportunities they can find there.

4. The impact _____ by individuals would be minimal.

5. The child could use the points _____ various virtual skills for the video game.

6. We have observed that there was a(n) _____ change about 4,100 years ago.

7. Trees have a remarkable ability _____ the air _____ removing harmful pollutants and filtering unwanted odours.

8. _____ from around 165,000 in 1992, the number of newly graduated students in Britain showed a(n) _____ rise in the next five years.

Exercise 2 根据提示,在横线上填入适当的单词或短语。（每空一词）

1. 大部分在市区街道穿梭(run)的机动车都会排放含有二氧化碳的尾气。

   A majority of vehicles _____ （非谓语动词作定语）on urban streets emit carbon dioxide from their exhausts.

2. 高额的医疗费用可能会限制病人对医生和药物的选择。

   The _____ （修饰词）medical expense may limit _____ （限定词）choice _____ _____ _____ _____ （介词短语）.

3. 公民可以购买私人保险来支付医疗费用。

Citizens can buy _____ (修饰词) insurance _____ _____ (非谓语动词作目的状语) the medical expenses.

4. 生活在多元社会的人们可以放心地和其他族群一起享用和分享家乡美食。

People _____ (非谓语动词作定语) in multicultural societies can openly enjoy and share their hometown cuisine _____ _____ _____ (介词短语).

5. 为了减少人口老龄化造成的不良影响, 制定有效的策略显得愈加有必要。

In order to mitigate the negative impact _____ (非谓语动词作定语) by ageing populations, it will be increasingly necessary to develop _____ (修饰词) strategies.

Exercise 3 请按中文意思扩充下列句子。

1. New Zealand is a country. 新西兰是一个国家。

扩1 新西兰是一个小国。

_____

扩2 新西兰是一个小国, 有 400 万居民。

_____

2. Mobile communication offers a way for us. 移动通信给我们提供了一种方式。

扩1 移动通信给我们提供了一种消磨 (pass) 时间的方式。

_____

扩2 移动通信给我们提供了在各种等待期间 (period) 消磨时间的方式。

_____

3. Coach launched the Poppy handbags. 蔻驰推出了 Poppy 系列手袋。

扩1 蔻驰推出了价格较低的 Poppy 系列手袋。

_____

扩2 凭借这些见解 (insight), 蔻驰推出了价格较低的 Poppy 系列手袋。

_____

4. Governments should continue to support athletes. 政府应该继续支持运动员。

扩1 政府应该继续支持专业运动员。

_____

扩2 政府应该建造专门的训练设施 (facilities), 以继续支持专业运动员。

_____

5. A city is a concrete jungle. 城市是水泥森林。

扩1 没有足够的绿化空间, 城市就是水泥森林。

_____

扩2 没有足够的绿化空间, 建满高层 (high-rise) 住宅楼的城市就是水泥森林。

_____

(答案见 pp. 120~121)

第2节　写出正确的并列句

一　并列句的3种连接方式

并列句（Compound Sentence）即把两个或以上的独立分句连接在一起而成的句子。

并列句的连接方式有三种：①利用并列连词（coordinator）连接；②利用分号和连接副词连接；③利用分号连接。

1. 利用并列连词连接

并列连词是用来表示分句之间并列关系的连词。并列句中各分句的关系是平行的，没有从属关系。但各分句之间却可以有不同的逻辑关系，分句之间的逻辑关系要靠不同的并列连词来表达。

结构	独立分句+, + 并列连词+独立分句
标点用法	并列连词前的独立分句要在句末加逗号；并列连词后不用逗号
并列连词	常用的有7个，分别是**for、and、nor、but、or、yet和so**，可根据首字母记作**FANBOYS**
例句	例 Sure, most of the produce is much cheaper, **but** a lot of it is not organically grown. 译 当然，大多数农产品都很便宜，但很多都不是有机种植的。

2. 利用分号和连接副词连接

连接副词可以用来连接分句，但需注意其前后标点符号的使用。

结构	独立分句+; + 连接副词+, +独立分句
标点用法	连接副词与前面的独立分句之间要用分号分隔；连接副词后要加逗号
连接副词及短语	除also、furthermore、moreover等连接副词外，也可用起过渡作用的副词短语，如on the other hand、as a result、for example等
例句	例 Currently, most cities in existence are classified as horizontal cities; **however,** the trend towards urban sprawl cannot be sustained indefinitely. 译 目前，大多数现存的城市都被划分为水平城市；然而，城市扩张的趋势不可能无限期地持续下去。

> **Tips**
>
> 在不使用分号的情况下，在连接副词前添加一个并列连词，也能连接两个分句。
>
> 例 Consequently, preventing climate changes would decrease the unpredictable effects, **and therefore** famine would be reduced.
>
> 译 因此，预防气候变化将减少其不可预测的影响，从而饥荒也会减少。

3. 利用分号连接

分号也能将两个独立分句连接起来，但要注意，只有当两个独立分句的语义非常紧密相关时，才可采取这种方式连接成并列句。否则，应写成两个独立的句子，皆以句号结尾。

例 Ultimately, both forms of charity work are essential; however, I believe that it is more important to address the issue of poverty within our own countries before looking beyond our borders to help the needy overseas.

译 最终的结论是，这两种形式的慈善工作都很重要；但是，我相信在跨越国界去帮助海外的贫困者之前，解决我们本国的贫困问题更重要。

二 常见的7个并列连词（FANBOYS）

前面提到，常用的并列连词有7个，分别是 **for**、**and**、**nor**、**but**、**or**、**yet**、**so**，以下是它们的具体用法。

并列连词	作用	例句
for 因为	引出原因	例 An interview may not be objective enough, **for** the selection of interview questions and the level of scrutiny can depend upon interviewers' personality and mood. 译 面试可能不够客观，因为面试问题的选择和审查的程度取决于面试官的性格和心情。
and 而且，并且	引出相似的、平等的内容	例 The cure for bad teaching is good teachers, **and** good teachers cost money. 译 解决教学质量差的办法就是请好的教师，而请好的教师是需要花钱的。
nor 也不	引出另一个否定的内容	例 In these cases, the criminal does not need education in the academic sense, **nor** does he/she require job skills. 译 在这些情况下，罪犯不需要学术上的教育，也不需要工作技能。
but 但是	引出相反的内容	例 Specifically, men are generally seen as the providers, **but** instead of going out to hunt for food, they go off to work to make money. 例 具体来说，男性通常被视为养家糊口的人，但他们不是外出打猎觅食，而是出去工作赚钱。
or 否则	引出另一种可能性	例 We must deal with the problem now, **or** it will be too late. 译 我们必须现在处理这个问题，否则就太晚了。
yet 然而	引出出人意料的内容	例 It is good, **yet** it could be improved. 译 它是好的，但它还有改善的空间。
so 所以	引出预料中的结果	例 Public transport is really dirty and inefficient, **so** many people prefer to use their cars. 译 公共交通很不干净，效率低下，所以很多人更喜欢使用自己的汽车。

Tips

1. nor相当于and not，用来连接两个否定的独立分句。注意nor后的分句要用倒装语序。

2. but和yet都可以引出相反的内容。当两个分句的内容是直接相反时，用but较为合适。当第二个分句的内容出乎人们的意料，含有"不应如此，怎么会这样"的意味时，用yet较为合适(实际上，but用在以上两种语境中均可接受，yet只有后一种意味，故写作时若不确定，可直接用but)。试比较：

例1 The company promises future improvements in tasks like networking, **but** applications are still a sore point. (直接相反的内容)

译1 该公司承诺未来将在联网等任务上进行改进，但应用程序仍然是一个痛点。

例2 It is impossible to describe Vietnam as having the most successful economy in the world, **yet** the happiest people are from that country, according to surveys. (出人意料的结果)

译2 越南远远不能说是世界上经济发展得最成功的国家，但据调查显示，最快乐的人就来自越南。

三 常见的连接副词及短语

在雅思写作中，连接副词和短语能够帮助说明句子之间的逻辑关系，使文章思路更加清晰，也更有条理。以下是常见的连接副词和短语的具体用法。

连接词	作用	例句
also/furthermore/ in addition/moreover 此外，另外	引出相似的、平等的内容	例 The problem is most ideas never get implemented, **and moreover**, even the best ideas when improperly implemented can cause great harm. 译 问题是大多数想法从未得到实施，而且，即使是最好的想法，如果实施不当也会造成巨大的伤害。
however/ nevertheless/ nonetheless/still 然而，不过	引出出人意料的内容	例 In my opinion, the arts are here to stay; **however**, the ways in which art is created and displayed will invariably be influenced by science and technology. 译 在我看来，艺术会持续存在；然而，艺术创作和展示的方式总是受到科技的影响。
on the other hand/ in contrast 另一方面；与此相反	引出相反的内容	例 It was an unfortunate experience, **but, on the other hand**, one can learn from one's mistakes. 译 这是一次不幸的经历，但另一方面，人们可以从错误中吸取教训。
otherwise 否则	引出另一种可能性	例 It is important to tighten up the wheels properly; **otherwise**, they vibrate loose and fall off. 译 把车轮拧紧很重要，否则它们会因振动而松脱。
accordingly/ consequently/ hence/therefore/ thus/as a result 因此	引出预料中的结果	例 In my view, children and adults cannot be seen as identical in the eyes of the law, **and therefore** age must be taken into account when punishing offenders. 译 在我看来，儿童和成人在法律上是不一样的，因此在惩罚罪犯时必须考虑到年龄。
for instance/ for example 例如	举例	例 What you eat can be contributory to certain illnesses; **for example**, a diet high in animal fats seems to be linked with coronary heart disease. 译 你吃的东西可能会导致某些疾病；例如，富含动物脂肪的饮食似乎与冠心病有关。

Exercise 1 选词填空。

1. Museums are really expensive, _____ (so/but) lots of people can't afford to go to there.

2. Due to humankind's huge population on the Earth, many animals' natural habitats have been destroyed, _____ (and/yet) many wild animals' prey is no longer sufficient in number to sustain them.

3. Some people think teaching children of different abilities together benefits all of them, _____ (or/but) others think intelligent children should be taught separately and given special treatment.

4. To conclude, as we can see, some of the schemes are flourishing, _____ (yet/nor) many are short of money and other essential resources.

5. If young people do not know about their cultural heritage, they will not understand the older generation; _____ (in addition/as a result), there could be serious communication breakdowns within cultures.

6. These issues have negative effects on healthcare and education; _____ (for example/as a consequence), my mother worries that she will not be able to cook healthy meals for her family if food costs continue to increase.

7. So we have to have a global plan; _____ (thus/otherwise), there's every possibility that there will be catastrophic consequences.

8. These qualities are not specific to men or women; _____ (therefore/still), both genders are able to raise children successfully.

9. A few years ago, visitors to a local park would see people who were playing football or walking their dog; _____ (hence/however), nowadays people are using the gym or a climbing wall as their way of sporting recreation.

10. First of all, people need changes; _____ (furthermore/nonetheless), we need obstacles to overcome and reach our goals.

Exercise 2 改正下列句子中的连接词错误。若没有错误，则用 C 标记。

1. We have not yet won; however, we shall keep trying.

2. Firstly, it is important to remember that this is an industry that develops incredibly rapidly; otherwise, it is difficult to make definite predictions.

3. It is estimated that agricultural yields will need to double by 2050, but climate change is a major threat to achieving this.

4. Of course, a company may lose a part of its profit, but security of its clients must be on the first place, yet clients will switch to another company and never be back.

5. Nobody would deny that a famous person works hard and is skilful because such people do not work any harder than thousands of other workers who have no claim to fame.

but	for example	in contrast	moreover	thus

1. First, swimming alone is against the rules.

Swimming alone is dangerous.

_____

_____

2. It cost the company a lot of money.

It saved the clients.

_____

_____

3. Children have some advantages living in a big city.

They have more opportunities to choose what they want to do.

_____

_____

4. The solution is for government to encourage the use of public transport in urban areas.

People will be less dependent on their cars.

_____

_____

5. Americans believed the next most important quality for men was ambition.

The next most important characteristic for women leaders was to be creative.

_____

_____

（答案见 pp. 121~122）

在雅思写作中，熟练准确地使用从句能够使我们对事物的描述和观点的表达更加具体，行文也更高级，为写作增分不少。

英语的从句主要有**定语从句**、**名词性从句**和**状语从句**这三大类。因此，本节将聚焦这三大类从句，总结归纳其正确的使用方法，以便大家能够合理地运用在写作中，展现自己的文章风采。

一 写出正确的定语从句

1. 定语从句的用处

定语从句本质上相当于一个形容词，用以修饰名词或代词，是将两个分句连接起来的方式之一。在雅思写作中，对信息进行限定或添加额外信息时，常需要用到定语从句。

例

There are many diseases, such as cancer.	**+**	These diseases are a result of living in the modern world and cannot be prevented by a healthy lifestyle.	**➡**	There are many diseases, such as cancer, **which** are a result of living in the modern world and **which** cannot be prevented by a healthy lifestyle.

译 有许多疾病，如癌症，是生活在现代世界的结果，不能通过健康的生活方式来预防。

析 例句中原来的两个句子都是结构完整的独立分句，但前一个短句很明显句意并不完整，读完后面的长句我们才知道短句所说的many diseases是指哪一类疾病。因此，可以把长句的These diseases用关系词which替代，整个句子变为短句中many diseases的定语从句，对其进行限定。由于从句有and连接的两个并列谓语，且关系词which都作其主语，所以which都不可省。

2. 定语从句的选用

定语从句可分为限制性定语从句（restrictive attributive clause）和非限制性定语从句（non-restrictive attributive clause）。两者在形式、作用和重要性上都有区别。

定语从句类别	形式	作用	重要性
限制性定语从句	无逗号	对修饰的内容进行**定义、解释**	从句的信息是**必要的**，若删去从句，整个句子信息不完整
非限制性定语从句	有逗号	进行**额外的补充说明**	从句的信息是**非必要的**，若删去，整个句子意思还是完整的

例1

Farmers in developing countries usually do not have enough money for measures.	**+**	The measures will help counteract the effects, for example anti-flooding or irrigation methods.	**➡**	Farmers in developing countries usually do not have enough money for measures **which** will help counteract the effects, for example anti-flooding or irrigation methods.

译1 发展中国家的农民通常没有足够的钱采取有助于抵消这些影响的措施，例如防洪方法或灌溉方法。

析1 在例句中，will help counteract the effects是对measures的限定信息，若没有这一信息，读者无法知道measures具体指什么措施，句子表意不明确。因此，此处要用限制性定语从句。

例2

| The problem requires a global effort and huge investment. | + | This is difficult to achieve quickly in the short term. | → | The problem requires a global effort and huge investment, **which** is difficult to achieve quickly in the short term. |

译2 这个问题需要全球的努力和大量的投资,这很难在短期内迅速实现。

析2 后面的句子是对前面句子所说情况的评论,即使去掉,也不影响读者对前一句的理解,所以后一句是非必要的补充信息,改为定语从句时使用非限制性定语从句这一形式。

Tips

非限制性定语从句常可替代and连接的并列分句。如果发现作文中用了过多and连接的并列句型,可以尝试将后半句转换为which/who引导的定语从句。

例 One important stage in a child's growth is certainly the development of a conscience, and it is linked to the ability to tell right from wrong.

改 One important stage in a child's growth is certainly the development of a conscience, **which** is linked to the ability to tell right from wrong.

译 儿童成长过程中的一个重要阶段无疑是良知的形成,这与辨别是非的能力相关。

析 原句是由and连接的并列句。由于后一分句的主语it指代的正是前一分句中的the development of a conscience,因此后一分句可以转换为which引导的非限制性定语从句,修饰the development of a conscience,句子意思不变。

3. 关系词的选用

定语从句需要由关系词引导,其作用有两个,一是连接主句和从句,二是替代被修饰的词(即先行词)。

关系词分为两种:**关系代词**和**关系副词**。关系代词在从句中充当主语、宾语或定语,关系副词则充当状语。

关系词的选用应根据定语从句的性质(限制性还是非限制性),以及先行词在从句中的成分(作主语、宾语还是其他)和性质(是人还是物)而定。具体如下:

关系代词				
	限制性定语从句		非限制性定语从句[1]	
功能	指代人	指代物	指代人	指代物
主语	who, that	which, that	who	which
宾语[2]	who, whom, that (可省略)	which, that (可省略)	who, whom	which
定语	whose	whose, of which	whose	whose, of which
关系副词				
功能	关系副词	"介词+which"的形式		被替代的先行词
时间状语	when	at/in/on/during etc.+which		表示时间的名词
地点状语	where	in/at etc.+which		表示地点的名词
原因状语	why(可省略)	for which		只有reason
方式状语	that(可省略)	in which		the way

注1:注意,that不能引导非限制性定语从句。

注2:当关系代词作介词宾语且介词出现在关系代词之前时,不用who和that,且不可省略。

4. 定语从句易错点

（1）注意避免成分的赘余

定语从句中，与关系词重复的部分要删掉，不必再写。

例 Firstly, art is an essential subject which children should learn it̶ in order to help promote their creativity and imagination.

译 首先，艺术是一门孩子必学的学科，以帮助提高他们的创造力和想象力。

析 在这个句子中，which引导的限制性定语从句修饰先行词subject。关系代词which指代subject，在从句中作learn的宾语，因此learn后面不需要再加it，否则会造成成分赘余。

（2）注意遵循主谓一致原则

定语从句的谓语单复数应根据先行词的单复数而定。定语从句修饰整个句子时，谓语动词用单数形式。

例 For example, panda is an endangered species which **has** been successfully bred in zoos, thus helping to keep the species alive.

译 例如，大熊猫是濒危物种，它们在动物园里成功得到培育，这从而有助于保持这个物种存活。

析 在这个句子中，which引导的限制性定语从句修饰先行词species，由an可知species在此处为单数意义，因此定语从句中的助动词have需要用第三人称单数形式，即has。

（3）注意关系词中的介词

当先行词在从句中作状语，关系词采用"介词+which"的形式时，注意不要遗漏介词。

例 Just look at the ways **in which** everything under the sun has been marketed.

译 看看天底下所有东西的营销方式。

析 在这个句子中，ways与in搭配在从句中充当状语，将其位置还原后为everything under the sun has been marketed **in the ways**，因此用which指代ways的定语从句中，需要保留介词in。

二 写出正确的名词性从句

1. 名词性从句的用处

名词性从句是在句子中起名词作用的从属分句，包括**宾语从句**、**主语从句**、**同位语从句**、**表语从句**。名词性从句在雅思写作中很常用，主要用于引出个人、他人、大众的观点，引出有争议的话题和提出质疑等。

例 ①It is true that many older people believe in traditional values that often seem incompatible with the needs of younger people. ② While I agree that some traditional ideas are outdated, I believe that others are still useful and should not be forgotten.

译 的确，许多老年人信奉传统价值观，而这些价值观似乎往往与年轻人的需求格格不入。虽然我同意有些传统观念已经过时，但我认为有些传统观念仍然有用，不应被遗忘。

析 句①利用主语从句复述题目，引出争议性话题。句②利用两个宾语从句引出个人观点。

在雅思写作中，在引出话题或观点时，常用"It+be+形容词/过去分词+that从句"这种句型，其中It为形式主语，真正的主语是后面的that从句。这种表达能使我们免于注明观点来源，也使文章更加客观。

例 Despite mixed opinions regarding whether or not it is necessary to travel overseas in order to learn about foreign cultures, **it can be argued that** it is possible to acquire cultural knowledge and understanding to varying degrees at home or abroad.

译 是否需要到海外去学习外国文化，人们意见不一，但可以说，在国内外都能从不同程度上去了解和理解他国文化。

2. 名词性从句的位置

（1）位于动词后

例 I **agree** that taking a parenting course can benefit both parents and children.

译 我认为参加育儿课程对父母和孩子都有益。

析 agree在此处为及物动词，因此后面that引导的从句为其宾语从句，属于名词性从句。此宾语从句用于引出个人的观点。

（2）位于介词后

例 The question **of** whether or not parents should be actively involved in children's literacy development is an issue worthy of debate.

译 家长是否应当主动参与到孩子读写能力的培养过程中，这个问题值得讨论。

析 whether引导的宾语从句放在介词of后面，充当了一个名词。在雅思写作中，"the question of+whether从句"这一结构常常出现，用来表述问题。

（3）位于形容词后

例 It is **crucial** that museum actively promote their upcoming exhibits in advance and clearly state the commencement times and dates.

译 博物馆有必要提前积极宣传最新展览，清楚告知开展的时间和日期。

析 这是典型的"It+be+形容词+that从句"句型，that从句为后置的主语从句。这种句型用于对某件事或某种做法发表评论。

（4）位于名词后

这类名词包括idea、theory、thought、claim、statement、assertion、belief、notion、opinion等。

例 My views may seem to ignore the **belief** that businesses should act in accordance with moral principles even if this leads to a reduction in their profits.

译 我的观点似乎忽略了这样一种信念，即企业应该按照道德准则行事，即使这会导致利润减少。

析 在雅思写作中，若我们想说明某一个名词的内容，也可以运用名词性从句（作同位语）。画线部分的从句，它与前面的名词belief是同位关系，说明belief的具体内容。

（5）位于句首

例 <u>Whether high level education or skills and experience are needed</u> depends on the position you apply for.

译 需要受教育水平高还是技能经验取决于你所申请的职位。

析 Whether引导主语从句，位于谓语动词depends on之前。注意主语由单个从句充当时，谓语动词使用第三人称单数形式。另外，表示"是否"的含义时，位于句首的主语从句只能用whether不能用if引导。

Tips

> 除了从句位于句首的情况，当从句位于介词后或者含有or not时，表示"是否"的引导词只能用whether，不能用if。另外，if一般不用于引导表语从句和同位语从句。
>
> 在写作中为了避免错误，可一律用whether引导名词性从句。

三 写出正确的状语从句

1. 状语从句的用处

状语从句的构成是"从属连词+分句"。在雅思写作中，状语从句也是高频使用的从句之一，可以用来引出话题，或者在论述观点的过程中用来提出假设、举例或讨论原因和结果等。

例1 **When** <u>it comes to learning about cultures other than one's own</u>, there is no match for travelling to the host destination and living amongst the locals.

译1 说到学习其他文化，没有什么比到东道国旅行并与当地人一起生活更好的了。

析1 When引导时间状语从句。when it comes to...是雅思写作中常用的句型，意为"当提及……的时候"，用于引出话题。

例2 **Although** <u>food advertising may have short-term effects on consumers by influencing their desire to buy and eat the advertised food product</u>, it is not directly responsible for excessive eating.

译2 虽然食品广告可能会对消费者产生短期影响，使他们想要购买和食用广告中的食品，但这并不是过度饮食的直接原因。

析2 在雅思写作中，如果想肯定相反观点的部分合理性令论述更充分，可以使用由although、though等引导的让步状语从句，来表达"尽管……，但是……"的意思。

例3 It may be very difficult for people to get medical attention **because** <u>there is a mountain between their village and the nearest hospital</u>.

译3 人们可能很难就医，因为他们的村庄和最近的医院之间有一座山。

析3 在雅思写作中，如果想要说明原因，可以使用由because、as等引导的原因状语从句。

例4 **If** <u>the factors identified above are implemented,</u> then any job can be improved and more workers can feel greater degrees of job satisfaction.

译4 如果上述因素得到贯彻，那么任何工作都可以得到改善，更多员工可以感受到更高程度的工作满意度。

析4 在雅思写作中，如果想要假设某一种情况来说明某件事情，则可以使用由if引导的条件状语从句。

2. 状语从句易错点

（1）误用标点符号

主句和从句位置是可以互换的，不影响意思。但要注意的是，如果从句放在主句之前，从句后要加逗号；如果从句放在主句之后，主从句之间不用加逗号。

例

When children are granted autonomy to take control of their own reading, they can choose the sources of reading material and read the things that are of most interest to them.	Children can choose the sources of reading material and read the things that are of most interest to them **when** they are granted autonomy to take control of their own reading.

（译）当孩子掌握了阅读的主动权，他们可以选择阅读材料的来源，阅读他们最感兴趣的东西。

（2）残缺句

状语从句必须依附于主句，不能独立成句。如果独立成句，就会形成残缺句。

例 It also requires a lot of concentration. **Because** you need to remember different steps and routines. ✗

It also requires a lot of concentration **because** you need to remember different steps and routines. ✓

（译）这还需要注意力高度集中，因为你需要记住不同的步骤和例程。

（3）连词混用

同学们受中文影响，在雅思写作中容易出现"因为"（because）和"所以"（so）一起使用，"虽然"（although）和"但是"（but）一起使用的错误。要注意，它们是不能在一个句子中共存的。

例 **Although** converting undeveloped land into residential housing may appear to be the logical step forward, **but** planting trees in these areas is arguably of far greater importance and a necessary long-term urban planning strategy. ✗

Although converting undeveloped land into residential housing may appear to be the logical step forward, planting trees in these areas is arguably of far greater importance and a necessary long-term urban planning strategy. ✓

Converting undeveloped land into residential housing may appear to be the logical step forward, **but** planting trees in these areas is arguably of far greater importance and a necessary long-term urban planning strategy. ✓

（译）虽然将未开发的土地转化为住宅看似是合理的发展措施，但在这些地方种植树木无疑更有意义，是必要的城市长远规划战略。

Exercise 1 在横线上填入适当的引导词。

1. Similarly, people _____ collect dolls may go beyond simply enlarging their collection and develop an interest in the way _____ dolls are made, or the materials _____ are used.

2. _____ many diseases that affect humans have been eradicated due to improvements in vaccinations and the availability of healthcare, there are still areas around the world _____ certain health issues are more prevalent.

3. _____ we imagine the act of storytelling, we often think of bedtime stories, _____ are generally read to children by their parents as a way of preparing the child for sleep.

4. Nevertheless, I maintain _____ fostering a society of young, independent readers is a worthy ideal.

5. There are those _____ are convinced _____ the harm caused to wildlife is irreversible.

6. Some people are of the opinion that foreign language learning should be compulsory _____ it helps intellectual development.

7. The charts give information about the activities in _____ U.K. bachelors and postgraduates participated after college graduation apart from full-time work in 2018.

8. The United Kingdom is a prime example, _____ money from smokers is used to treat lung cancer and heart disease.

Exercise 2 改正下列句子中的错误。

1. Banks work to improve customer confidence, which they rely on it for their business.

2. Many countries don't have the money for desalination plants, which is very expensive to build.

3. Natural resources often become overexploited, when places of interest are overcrowded.

4. Nowadays, although tourism generates a significant portion of national income for many countries, but it has certain drawbacks too.

5. In conclusion, because many wild animals' natural habitats have been destroyed by humans, so we can do our best to make their manmade environments in zoos as spacious and natural as possible.

Exercise 3 根据括号内的要求改写句子。

1. The bar chart gives information about the percentages of both men and women. The men and women consumed five types of fruits and vegetables each day in Britain. (使用限制性定语从句合并句子)

_____

_____

2. We can see that manufacture of olive oil is a complex process involving many steps and many devices. (使用主语从句改写句子)

_____

3. This will mean that some people are unable to afford healthcare. That is why I disagree with the user-pays system. (使用非限制性定语从句合并句子)

_____

4. People see or hear a well-known figure asking for their help. They are more likely to make a donation or volunteer their time to furthering the charity's work. (使用时间状语从句合并句子)

_____

5. We will come to rely on machines to complete dangerous or repetitive tasks to an even greater extent soon. This is foreseeable. (使用主语从句合并句子)

_____

Exercise 4 翻译下列句子。

1. 可以看出,褐煤产生的能源损耗比黑煤稍高一些。

_____

2. 在21世纪,越来越多的人在能负担得起的情况下选择独居。

_____

3. 该表格对比了2012年和2017年澳大利亚各类住所的居民比例。

_____

4. 尽管回收利用耗费金钱和时间,但这是一个保护环境免受进一步破坏的方法。

_____

5. 没有证据证明禁止某类食品广告可以让全球人口的过度饮食率(the rate of overeating)显著下降。

_____

(答案见 pp. 122~124)

在雅思写作中，被动句是常用的写作句式，它既可以用来替换一些主动句，增加句式的多样性，又可以用来表达很多主动语态无法表达的内容。因此，用好被动句是雅思作文得高分的关键。

一　被动句的结构

英语语态分为两种：**主动语态**和**被动语态**。

被动语态用来表示动作与主语之间的被动关系，也就是中文里面的"被……"或"由……"句式。

被动句的结构：**be done+(by+ 动作执行者)**。其中，be 的形式随着时态和主语人称的单复数而变化。

常用时态中被动句的写法如下：

时态	结构	例句
一般现在时	is/am/are done	例 We **are told** that we ought to organise our company, our home life, our week, our day and even our sleep, all as a means to becoming more productive. 译 我们被告知，我们应该安排好我们的公司、我们的家庭生活、我们的一周、我们的一天,甚至我们的睡眠,所有这些都是为了提高生产力。
一般过去时	was/were done	例 The play **was written** to celebrate an anniversary. 译 这出戏是为周年纪念而写的。
一般将来时	will be done	例 The performance **will be attended** by officials from the town. 译 镇政府官员将出席观看这场表演。
现在进行时	is/am/are being done	例 This is an important source of timber for building houses and **is** increasingly **being used** as a replacement for endangered hardwoods in the furniture construction industry. 译 这是重要的建筑木材来源,并且越来越多地被用在家具建造业中,替代濒临灭绝的硬木。
现在完成时	has/have been done	例 Boredom proneness **has been linked** with a variety of traits. 译 无聊倾向与多种品质有关。
过去进行时	was/were being done	例 By 1990, 94 per cent of children **were being vaccinated** against whooping cough. 译 到1990年,94%的儿童接种了百日咳疫苗。
过去完成时	had been done	例 It contained technology that **had been developed** for the sports industry. 译 它包含了为体育产业开发的技术。
将来完成时	will/would have been done	例 By 2040, it is expected that there will be 1,000 pupils, and a third building **will have been constructed**. 译 到2040年,预计将有1,000名学生,届时第三栋建筑已建成。

二 被动句的用处

被动句是雅思写作中的常用句式，但这也不意味着被动句用得越多越好，被动句一般会在以下几种情况中使用。

1. 省略动作执行者

当我们不知道是谁执行了动作，或动作的执行者是谁并不重要时，可以使用被动句。

例1 As the third building and a second car park **will be built** on the site of the original sports field, a new, smaller sports field **will need to be laid**.

译1 由于第三栋建筑和第二个停车场将建在原来操场的位置上，因此需要铺设一个新的、小一点的操场。

析1 在这个句子中有两个被动语态，分别是 will be built 和 will need to be laid，两个动作的执行者都不是特定的或需要强调的某一个人，因此句子没有用主动语态表示"谁干了什么"，而是用被动语态告诉读者"什么被怎么样"。

例2 In the past, such children **were considered** to be at a disadvantage compared with their monolingual peers.

译2 在过去，与单语同龄人相比，这些孩子被认为处于劣势。

析2 在这个句子中，读者关注的是"孩子被认为处于劣势"这一现象，而不是被"谁"认为。

2. 客观呈现观点、意见

例1 If a citizen is unhealthy and weak, it **can be assumed** that that individual is not contributing his or her potential energy, optimum work abilities and knowledge to his or her community.

译1 如果一个公民身体不健康且虚弱，可以认为这个人无法为其社区贡献自己的潜在能量、最佳工作能力和知识。

析1 句型 It can be assumed that... 表示"可以认为……"。It是形式主语，替代的是后面that引导的从句。这个句型一来避免了主语太长，二来模糊了观点持有者，突出了观点，此时被动语态的使用是为客观呈现观点、意见而服务的。

例2 It **is thought** that the proportion of elderly people will be similar in the three countries.

译2 人们认为，这三个国家的老年人比例会很接近。

析2 句型 It is thought that 表示"人们认为……"。同样这里的It也是形式主语，真正的主语是后面that引导的从句。这个句子使用被动语态突出观点，而不是突出观点持有者，使文章的论述更客观。

1. 用被动语态表达观点的常用句型还有"**It is said/believed/reported/announced that+ 从句**"，一般翻译为"有人说/人们相信/据报道/据称……"。

2. 在雅思小作文中，常用 expect、project 和 predict 的被动态描述将来的数据。例如：Overall sales **are predicted** to be over 5,000 in the next decade."预计未来十年的总销量将超过5,000辆。"

3. 强调动作执行者

当我们想要强调动作的执行者时，可以使用 "be done by+ 动作执行者" 的句式。

例1 Repetitive manual jobs **are** now **done by** machine.

译1 重复的体力劳动现在由机器来完成。

析1 在这个句子中，关键信息是"谁"完成重复的体力劳动，被动句中的by让读者的注意力自然放在了这个动作的执行者machine上。

例2 Student-driven learning **is facilitated by** teachers' encouragement.

译2 学生自主学习需要老师的鼓励来促进。

析2 这个句子用is facilitated by这一被动句结构，可以让读者清晰地看到学生自主学习需要什么，突出老师鼓励的重要性。

三 被动句易错点

1. 时态不一致

当主动语态变成被动语态时，其谓语动词的时态要与原句时态保持一致。

例1
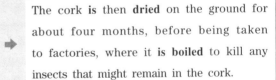

主动语态	被动语态
People then **dry** the cork on the ground for about four months, before taking it to factories, where they **boil** it to kill any insects that might remain in the cork.	The cork **is** then **dried** on the ground for about four months, before being taken to factories, where it **is boiled** to kill any insects that might remain in the cork.

译1 软木在地上晾干大约四个月后被送到工厂，在那里用沸水清洗以杀死可能残留在软木中的昆虫。

析1 主动句中的谓语动词dry和boil的时态为一般现在时，故改为被动句时，应保持时态的一致，分别改为is dried和is boiled。

例2
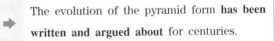

主动语态	被动语态
People **has written and argued about** the evolution of the pyramid form for centuries.	The evolution of the pyramid form **has been written and argued about** for centuries.

译2 有关金字塔形式演变的论述和争论已持续了几个世纪。

析2 主动句的时态为现在完成时，故改为被动句时，应保持时态的一致，用has been written and argued about。

2. 不及物动词使用被动语态

不及物动词如 happen、remain、lie、belong (to)、take place、break out 等没有被动语态。

例1 And it might not be a big change, but if it **happens** every day, it all adds up.

译1 这可能不是一个大的变化，但如果它每天都发生，那么就会积少成多。

析1 happen是不及物动词，也就是说它后面不能加宾语，所以不能使用被动语态。

例2 Concepts of wisdom may depend on the society we **belong to**.

译2 智慧的概念可能取决于我们所属的社会。

析2 belong是不及物动词, belong to sb./sth.意为"属于某人/某物", 也没有"被属于"这一个说法, 因此不能使用被动语态。

3. "主动表被动"的动词使用被动语态

部分动词如 taste、look、seem、sound、feel、sell 等用主动形式表示被动意义。

例1 The problems that **look** or **sound** most dramatic may not be the best places to start.

译1 看起来或听起来最引人注目的问题可能不是最好的着手点。

析1 虽然问题是"被看到"或"听到", 但是这里想要表达的是"一个怎么样的问题", 描述的是问题的性质, 它不会因为看到或听到的人不同而改变。因此, 当我们在描述某样东西"看起来""听起来"的特征时, 都用主动形式。

例2 Because food that is high in calories **tastes** better, and so they will **sell** more.

译2 因为热量高的食物味道更好, 所以它们会卖得更多。

4. 遗漏短语动词中的小品词

将主动句变为被动句时, 由"动词 + 介词 / 副词"组合成的短语动词, 要视为一个整体, 介词或副词不可以拆开或省略。

例

主动语态	被动语态
We can **think of** episodic memory as a process with several different steps of memory processing: encoding, consolidation and retrieval.	Episodic memory can **be thought of** as a process with several different steps of memory processing: encoding, consolidation and retrieval.

译 情景记忆可以被认为是一个具有几个不同记忆处理步骤的过程: 编码、巩固和检索。

析 在改写这个主动句时, 大家往往容易漏掉介词of, 尤其是当be thought of后面还有一个介词as的时候, 很容易根据中文意思"被认为"写成be thought as。为了避免这种情况, 我们要先观察主动句中的带有介词或副词的短语动词, 在改写成被动句时, 将它们完整保留下来。因此, 在这个例句中, think of这一短语动词中的介词of要保留, 改为be thought of。

小试牛刀

Exercise 1 写出下列动词的过去分词。

write	_____	invite	_____	cause	_____
damage	_____	take	_____	invent	_____
cut	_____	grow	_____	attend	_____
set	_____	bring	_____	construct	_____
think	_____	catch	_____	blow	_____
steal	_____	break	_____	freeze	_____
choose	_____	forget	_____	wake	_____
know	_____	rise	_____	mistake	_____

Exercise 2 将下列句子改为被动句。

1. Someone gives advice on selling photographs.

   Advice _____ on selling photographs.

2. The professor has written many books on the subject of study skills for students.

   Many books _____ on the subject of study skills for students by the professor.

3. People had converted the small road into a main road and extended it to the east.

   The small road _____ into a main road and extended to the east.

4. In total, people took an estimated 200,000 animals from the archipelago before the 20th century.

   In total, an estimated 200,000 animals _____ from the archipelago before the 20th century.

5. In all sorts of professions — whether artist, marine biologist or astronomer — people are testing borders of the unknown each day.

   In all sorts of professions — whether artist, marine biologist or astronomer — borders of the unknown _____ each day.

Exercise 3 改正下列句子中的错误。若没有错误，则用 C 标记。

1. It claims that the government funding for university should not use for purposes other than scholarships for the most outstanding students.

2. Since then, around 25 hotspots have identified as main targets for conservation.

3. Others believe the money should spend on improving existing public transport.

4. The field of health geography is often overlooked, but it is constituted a huge area of need in the fields of geography and healthcare.

5. Indeed, the closing decades of the 20th century were a time when it was seemed that anything could be turned into a commodity.

6. Firstly, its traditional image is more in keeping with that of the type of high-quality goods with which it has long associated.

7. Display homes are usually offered by major project builders who work on a large scale and can deliver good quality and value.

8. This is required an understanding of what motivates employees at different levels of management and different stages of their careers.

9. There is an argument that exploring space is a waste of money and that there are more urgent needs to be addressed on earth, such as reducing poverty and preventing environmental destruction.

10. While there is evidence to suggest that some babies born with genes that make them more prone to commit crimes, everybody ultimately has the power to decide whether or not to break the law.

Exercise 4 根据括号内的提示词，使用被动句翻译下列句子。

1. 自2013年以来，有更多关于该主题的论文已经被发表。(publish)

_____

2. 多种食品现在可以自由配送到世界各地。(distribute to)

_____

3. 然而，很多不可生物降解的(non-biodegradable)消费品是可回收利用的或是有可能循环利用到其他消费品上的。(recycle, reuse)

_____

4. 许多年轻人认为在手机或者平板电脑上阅读和写作更加快捷方便。(regard)

_____

5. 可以看出，印度、印度尼西亚和中国的受抚养人(dependant)比例高于世界平均水平。(observe)

_____

6. 我仍然坚持认为教师在教育中扮演的角色至关重要，不可忽视。(ignore)

_____

7. 有证据显示，个人往往会受到他们所看广告的负面影响。(affect)

_____

8. 显然，在1965年，高架桥主要是由私家车和公共交通使用。(use)

_____

9. 已有人建议，降低死亡人数和提高道路安全的最佳方法是提高取得驾照的最低年龄。（suggest）

_____

10. 尽管其他像抽烟那样的危害社会的行为目前在大部分公众场所都已经禁止，但我认为人们在公共场合有权利不受限制地自由使用手机。(prohibit)

_____

（答案见 pp. 124~125）

第3章 如何使句子出彩

语法多样性及准确性（Grammatical Range and Accuracy）是雅思写作的四大评分标准之一。

其中，语法准确性（Grammatical Accuracy）是指文章中不出现语法错误，或出现的语法错误不会影响阅卷者的理解。关于语法准确性的知识点在本册前两章已有详细的说明，本章内容将围绕提高语法多样性展开。

句子是雅思作文评分中非常关键的一个层面。好的句子能够丰富表达，同时让文章脉络显得清晰，使论述更有力。因此，在日常的练习中，有针对性地提升写好句的能力，能帮助我们的雅思作文获得更高分。

第1节 使用多变的句式

要增强句子的多样性，最直接的方法是使用多变而出彩的句式。

一 句子开头的6种方式

灵活地运用不同的句子开头方式，可以使我们的句型更丰富，写作语言更生动，从而增加语法多样性。

1. 以 it 开头的句子

英语句子成分常见的一种排列方式为"主语+谓语+宾语"，此处的主语通常是真实的主语。然而，当真实的主语为不定式短语、动名词短语或主语从句等较长的内容时，直接放置在句首会显得句子头重脚轻。此时，我们可以将it作为形式主语放在句子的开头，然后将真正的主语移到句子的末尾，以达到句子的平衡。

在雅思写作中，以形式主语 it 开头的句子很常见，具体句型如下。

（1）It+be+形容词+to do sth. "做某事是……的"

该句型描述事情的性质，常用来表达观点。

常用的形容词有：easy "简单的"，difficult "困难的"，important "重要的"，possible "可能的"，necessary "必要的"，wonderful "很棒的"。

例 **It is** almost **impossible to cook** something that everyone would like.

译 几乎很难做出每个人都喜欢的食物。

析 在这个句子中，真正的主语to cook something that everyone would like很长，如果将它放在句首，则显得头重脚轻。然而，用形式主语It代替真正的主语，能使句子开头看起来更轻巧，行文更流畅。此外，将重要的观点"impossible"放在前面，能够起到突出的效果，使写作的逻辑更清晰。

（2）It+be+形容词+that从句 "某事是……的"

该句型与第一种相似，同样常用于陈述观点、看法或者事实。

常用的形容词有：necessary "必要的"，important "重要的"，clear "清晰的"，obvious "明显的"，likely "可能发生的"，essential "非常重要的"。

例 **It is clear that** there are a range of other factors that threaten the safety of all road users.

译 显然还有很多其他因素会危及所有道路使用者的安全。

析 在这个句子中，真正的主语that there are... all road users很长，将它放在句首，会显得整个句子不协调。因此，使用形式主语It作为开头，显得句子更为平衡，也更能突出作者的观点。

（3）It+be+名词+to do sth. "做某事是……"

　　该句型常用于表示人们对于某件事情的定义或者看法。

　　常用的名词有：duty "责任"，pleasure "快乐"，honour "荣誉"。

例 **It is part of the duty** as cadres **to help** the masses.

译 帮助群众是干部应分的事。

析 运用It作为形式主语，从结构上突出了duty。

（4）It+be+名词+doing sth. "做某事是……的"

　　该句型也常用于表示人们对于某件事情的定义或者看法，常与含否定意义的名词短语搭配使用。

　　常用的名词短语有：no good "没用的，不适合的"，no use "没用的，无益的"。

例 **It is no use serving up** TV dinners if the kids won't eat them.

译 如果孩子们不肯吃，就是端上即食便餐也没有什么用。

析 It is no use doing sth. 表示 "做某事是没用的"，这个固定搭配在雅思写作中常用来表达观点。

（5）It+be+名词+that从句 "某事是……"

　　在雅思写作中，这也是陈述观点、看法或者事实的常用句型。

　　常用的名词短语有：a fact "事实"，a pity "遗憾"，a shame "耻辱"，an honour "荣誉"，a wonder "奇迹"，one's belief "某人的信念/想法"，good news "好消息"，no wonder "难怪"。

　　惯用表达有：

　　It is a surprise that... 令人惊讶的是……

　　It is a fact that... 事实上……

　　It is no wonder that... 难怪……

例 **It is my belief that** the incidence of many illnesses and diseases can be lowered to a great extent if governments all over the world are willing to enforce appropriate measures.

译 我相信，如果全世界的政府都愿意实施恰当的措施，许多疾病的发生率都能大幅下降。

析 It is my belief that相当于I believe that...，两个句型交换使用可增加文章句子的多样性。

（6）It+be+过去分词+that从句 "人们认为……"

　　雅思写作中，在引出别人或大众观点时，常用这个句型。

　　常用的动词（需改写成过去分词形式）有：believe "相信"，prove "证明"，argue "争辩"，agree "同意"。

例 **It could be argued that** governments should adopt a more proactive approach to eliminating preventable illnesses and diseases by addressing associated pollution and housing problems.

译 有人认为政府应该解决相关的污染和住房问题，这是消除可预防疾病更为积极的方法。

析 "It+be+argued that..."是一个在雅思写作中很常用的句型，尤其多用在文章开头，表明大多数人的观点。这种句型也可以写成主动语态，如此例句可写成Many people could argue that...，但It句型的使用更为普遍，也能更客观地说明观点。

（7）It takes+名词+(for sb.) to do sth. "（某人）做某事需要……"

　　该句型常用于表示做某事需要耗费的时间、金钱或条件等。

例 **It takes** time, effort and money **to** organise, build trust and **to** experiment.

译 组织、建立信任和试验需要时间、努力和金钱。

2. 副词开头

位于开头的副词，可以起到修饰整个句子或者限定范围的作用。

（1）副词修饰全句

当使用副词修饰全句的时候，这些副词大多数表示作者对句子内容的看法。

修饰全句常用的副词有：obviously"显然"，apparently"显然"，undoubtedly"无疑"，fortunately"幸运的是"，clearly"显而易见"，incredibly"令人难以置信的是"，surprisingly"出乎意料地"，frighteningly"可怕的是"。

例 **Unfortunately**, globalisation necessitates venturing into the most remote areas in order to experience foreign culture in its unadulterated form.

译 不幸的是，由于全球化，要体验原汁原味的异域文化，就得踏足最偏僻的地区。

析 Unfortunately 是一个副词，意思是"不幸的是"。将其放在句首，可以清晰地表明作者对于本句所述事件的看法和态度。

（2）副词表示某一领域，限定讨论角度

这类副词包括 financially"经济上"、traditionally"传统上"、historically"历史上"等。

例 **Financially**, many competitors are seriously disadvantaged simply because they come from poorer countries that cannot afford to support their training.

译 从经济上看，许多选手就是因为来自较为贫穷的国家，没有足够的资金支持他们的训练，而明显处于劣势。

析 Financially 放在句首，表明了这句话讨论问题的角度——经济方面，起到了限定和强调的作用。

3. 介词短语开头

介词短语放在句子开头，可以直观地表示时间、地点、方式、原因、条件等因素。

常用的介词有：in"在里面"，on"在上面"，for"为了"，by"通过"，without"没有"，with"有；用；随着"，around"在周围"，besides"除……之外"，despite"尽管"，before"在之前"，due to"由于"，because of"因为"，in case of"假使"，apart from"除了"，thanks to"由于，幸亏"。

例1 **Thanks to** the influence of westernisation and global spread of products and services, we can buy the brands we know and love no matter where we are in the world.

译1 得益于西方化以及商品和服务全球化的影响，不管我们在世界的哪个角落，我们都能买到我们熟悉且喜爱的牌子。

例2 **Despite** the downsides of world uniformity, I believe the advantages of a global culture outweigh the disadvantages.

译2 尽管世界一体化存在弊端，但我认为全球性文化的利大于弊。

4. 动名词短语开头

把动名词短语放在句子开头，常常用于引出一个话题或者事件，是让句式多变的一种手段。

例1 **Endeavouring** to exercise regularly is a constant struggle for many people, especially those living in large urban environments.

译1 对很多人来说，特别是住在大城市里的人，努力定期锻炼身体是一个长期的难题。

析1 这个句子以动名词短语 Endeavouring to exercise regularly 作为主语放在开头，直接引出了"努力定期锻炼身体"这个话题。由于此短语不算太长，因此无须使用 it 作形式主语。直接用动名词作主语，简洁明了，重点突出。

例2 **Accessing** information on any subject imaginable with just the click of a button is now possible thanks to the world's largest knowledge storehouse—the Internet.

译2 有了世界上最大的知识库——互联网，简单点击按钮就能获得任何一个能想到的事物的信息。

析2 这个句子以动名词短语Accessing information on any subject imaginable with just the click of a button作为主语放在开头，直观地表达了较为复杂的句意。本句中的主语虽然很长，但没有使用it作形式主语，这是因为本句后面的状语同样很长，即使不用形式主语代替真正主语，也不会显得句子头重脚轻。此外，稍长的主语和状语分布在句首和句尾，一头一尾，形成了微妙的平衡和对称之美。

5. 惯用语开头

雅思写作常用的惯用语有：

in other words 换句话说

in my opinion/from my perspective 我认为

in fact/as a matter of fact 实际上

in contrast/on the contrary 正相反

all in all/in a word/in conclusion/in summary 总之

more often than not/in general 通常

例1 **In my opinion**, charity organisations must assist their own local residents before contemplating directing funds elsewhere around the world.

译1 我认为慈善机构在考虑给世界其他地区提供资金之前，必须先援助本地居民。

析1 句子以In my opinion开头，引出作者自己的观点。

例2 **In contrast**, there is a tendency for celebrities to sometimes steal the limelight with the intention of increasing their own popularity.

译2 相反，有时候名人往往会借此抢风头，就为了提高自己的知名度。

析2 In contrast的意思是"相反地"，是常见的表示对比的短语。此句以其作为开头，清晰地表明了与前文的逻辑关系，使文章更连贯。

6. 从句开头

在雅思写作中，从句是很重要的句型组成部分，使用频率也很高。一般情况下，主句在前，从句在后。然而，在复合句里，除了位置比较固定的名词性从句和定语从句之外，我们可以灵活调整主句和从句的位置，将从句放到主句之前，从而突出写作重点，也能增加句式的多样性。这类从句主要是各种状语从句，如时间状语从句、条件状语从句、地点状语从句等。

例1

| They lose their entitlement to welfare <u>when they start work</u>. | | <u>When they start work</u>, they lose their entitlement to welfare. |

译1 他们一开始工作就失去了享受福利的权利。

析1 这句调整的是when引导的时间状语从句的位置，原句为"主句在前，从句在后"的结构。将该句的从句提前作开头后，从句部分的内容就被强调了，突出了"他们一开始工作"的时间点。

例2

| The individual is not exempt from any responsibility <u>although these factors provide compelling evidence in opposition of expanding university</u>. | | <u>Although these factors provide compelling evidence in opposition of expanding university</u>, the individual is not exempt from any responsibility. |

译2 虽然这些因素为反对高校扩招提供了强有力的证据，但个人也难辞其咎。

析2 这句调整的是让步状语从句的位置，同样是把从句提前，放在开头，强调了让步的内容。

虽然有这么多种句子开头的方式，但同学们要注意，具体选择哪一种要根据句意和表达重点而定。在写具体句子的时候，不必拘泥于某种句式，流畅的、表意清晰的句子开头方式即是好的。

[例] | Artists have alternative financial sources, like doing part time jobs. Alternative financial sources are available to artists like doing part time jobs.

[译] 艺术家还有别的经济来源，如做兼职。

[析] 为了突出"别的经济来源"，改写后的句子把原句的宾语 alternative financial sources 提前到句首，并使用了 be available to sb. "某人可获得……"的表达，这种写法也值得同学们参考。

二 使用倒装句

在英语中，句子的自然语序是主语在前，谓语动词在后。但有时由于句子结构的需要或表示强调，句子要采用倒装形式。倒装分为**完全倒装**和**部分倒装**两种。

正确地运用倒装句，可以起到强调的作用，使写作的句式更丰富，语言更生动，从而增加文章的语法多样性。

1. 完全倒装

在句子中，把完整的谓语动词提到主语前面的倒装结构被称为"完全倒装"。这类倒装句的谓语通常是 be、appear、seem 等系动词和 come、go 等不及物动词。以下为雅思写作中经常使用到的一些完全倒装结构。

（1）here 和 there 位于句首时的倒装

表示地点的 here 和 there 位于句首时，其后用完全倒装形式。其中，一个特殊的例子是雅思写作中很常见的 There be 句型。There be 句型是英语中陈述客观事物存在的常用句型，其意思为"有"，通常用于表示"某个地方存在着某物或某人"。There 在句中为引导词，没有具体的含义。

[例1] **There is** another staircase in the southwestern corner of the dormitory building.

[译1] 在宿舍楼的西南角还有一个楼梯。

[析1] 这是一个 There be 句型的完全倒装句。在这个例子中，正常的语序应该为"Another staircase in the southwestern corner of the dormitory building is there."。主语 another staircase in the southwestern corner of the dormitory building 较长，若放在句首，句子显得头重脚轻。使用 There be 句型进行倒装，句子的结构更合理，表达也更为地道。

[例2] **There seem to be** two main attitudes toward that question.

[译2] 对于这个问题，似乎主要有两种态度。

[析2] 这也是一个 There be 句型，只是 be 动词前加了半助动词 seem to。正常的语序应该为"Two main attitudes toward that question seem to be there."。

（2）介词短语作状语位于句首时的倒装

在写作中，为了强调，我们可以将作状语的介词短语放在句首，将主语放到句末，形成完全倒装。采用这种倒装结构有时也是出于全句平衡的考虑，当句子的主语较长时，我们常以作状语的介词短语开头，避免头重脚轻。

[例] **Behind the retreat from the plan** *lies* a belief that, in fiscally tough times, costs are better controlled from the centre.

[译] 计划改变的原因是，政府相信，在财政困难时期，成本由中央控制更好。

析 这个句子正常的语序应该为 "A belief that, in fiscally tough times, costs are better controlled from the centre lies behind the retreat from the plan."。使用倒装，可以强调状语Behind the retreat from the plan。同时，将原句中较长的主语a belief that... from the centre放置在句子末端，避免了句子头重脚轻的情况，有利于句子平衡。

（3）表语位于句首时的倒装

当表示地点、位置、范围、处所的表语被提前至句首时，句子使用完全倒装。

例1 **Among them** is the target of bringing down all of Northern Ireland's peace walls by 2023.

译1 其中包括了到2023年拆除北爱尔兰所有和平墙的目标。

析1 这个句子正常的语序应该为 "The target of... by 2023 is among them."。句子倒装后，表范围的表语Among them被提前至句首，起到了强调的作用，句子首尾也更平衡。

主语较长或结构较复杂的句子，常将表语置于句首，这时要用完全倒装。

例2 **Gone** *are* the days when work was just a stopgap between leaving school and getting married.

译2 把工作当成毕业和结婚的过渡期的日子已经一去不复返了。

析2 这个句子正常的语序应该为 "The days when work... and getting married are gone."。这句话的主语the days由于带有一个when引导的定语从句，整个部分较长，使用倒装可以平衡句子结构。

2. 部分倒装

在句子中，把谓语的一部分（助动词或情态动词）提到主语前面的倒装结构被称为"部分倒装"。以下为雅思写作中经常使用到的一些部分倒装结构。

（1）so... that句型的部分倒装

在so... that句型中，我们有时要强调so所修饰的形容词或副词，就将so连同它所修饰的形容词或副词一起提到句首。这时，主句要用部分倒装结构。

例 **So well** *did* these hired hands *do* **that** they recouped most of their costs.

译 这些雇工做得非常好，他们收回了大部分成本。

析 在这个句子中，为了强调so所修饰的副词well，主句So well did these hired hands do使用了部分倒装，把助动词did提到主语these hired hands前，实义动词do变成原形，其正常语序为These hired hands did so well that...。

（2）句首为否定词或含否定意义的词语时的部分倒装

句首为否定词或含否定意义的词语时，句子要部分倒装。此时的句子结构为：否定词+助动词/系动词be+主语（+谓语）+其他成分。若句子的谓语为系动词be，且不带有助动词，则把be动词提前至主语前，主语后直接跟其他成分。

此类否定词有：

全部否定	no 没有	not 不	never 从不	neither 也不	nor 也不
部分否定	seldom/rarely 很少		barely/scarcely/hardly 几乎不		

例 **Never** *did* they *contemplate* the world of apps, which just surpassed 70 billion downloads.

译 他们从未考虑过应用程序的世界，应用程序的下载量已突破700亿次。

（3）句首为Only时的部分倒装

句首为Only,后接状语时,句子(或主句)要使用部分倒装。此时的句子结构为: Only+状语+助动词/系动词be+主语(+谓语)+其他成分。若句子的谓语为系动词be,且不带有助动词,则把be动词提前至主语前,主语后直接跟其他成分。

例 **Only** when each of us realizes the importance of water, *can* we *live* a better life.

译 只有当我们每个人都意识到水的重要性,我们才能过上更好的生活。

析 在此句中,主句的正常语序应该为we can live a better life。当Only修饰状语放在句首时,其后的主句要使用部分倒装结构,将情态动词can提前,变成can we live a better life。这个例子中,Only修饰的时间状语从句提前,强调了"当我们每个人都意识到水的重要性"是"我们过上更好的生活"的必要前提。在写作中,句首为Only的部分倒装句型能够突出Only所修饰的状语的内容(一般为做某事的前提或条件)。

（4）使用not only... but (also)结构时的部分倒装

在句子中使用not only... but (also)结构时,若not only后面为完整的并列分句,该分句要进行部分倒装。

例 **Not only** *did* they *lose* their jobs, **but** they lost a pension they thought was guaranteed.

译 他们不仅失去了工作,还失去了本以为有保障的养老金。

析 此句使用了部分倒装,其正常语序为 "They not only lost their jobs, but also lost a pension they thought was guaranteed."。

在平时的语言积累和写作练习中,我们可以多模仿这几种固定句型,掌握一些倒装句的基本写法。在雅思写作时,适当使用倒装句,能让语言表达更丰富灵活,增强文章的语法多样性。

三 使用强调语气

强调语气的作用是突出句子的某一部分,以此表明语句的重点,引起读者的注意。下面是使用强调语气的几种方式。

1. 在谓语动词前加 do

如果要对谓语动词进行强调,只需在谓语动词前加上相应时态的助动词do即可。

例 I **do** believe in people being able to do what they want to do, providing they are not hurting someone else.

译 我确实相信人们可以做他们想做的事,只要他们不伤害他人。

析 在这个例句中,主要谓语动词believe前加do对该动作表示强调,凸显作者坚定的立场。在雅思写作中,同学们也可以用 "I do believe (that)" 这个句式来强调自己的观点。

2. 使用形容词或副词

在句子中恰当地使用形容词和副词,也能起到强调的作用。

常用的形容词有very"正是的";副词有very"非常",ever"以往任何时候",only"只有"。

例 That's the **very** thing I need.

译 那正是我需要的东西。

析 在这个例子中,very作为形容词,用来修饰名词thing,强调"正是那一个"。在雅思写作中,very修饰名词的情况并不罕见,同学们可以学着使用。

3. 双重否定

例 It is **not uncommon** for college students to live at home.

译 大学生住在家里并不少见。

析 在这个例子中，not和uncommon同时使用，构成了双重否定的结构，其意思为"不是不寻常的"，即"很普遍"。这种写法比直接肯定更让人印象深刻。

4. 使用 what 引导的主语从句

若想强调句子的主语或宾语，可以改写为"what从句+be..."结构，what指代所强调的成分，be动词后则是强调的具体内容。

常见的句型有：

What matters is... 重要的是……

What attracts me most is... 最吸引我的是……

例 **What matters** for most scientists **is** money and facilities.

译 对大多数科学家来说，重要的是经费和设备。

析 正常的语序是"For most scientists, money and facilities matter."。这个例句利用What matters... is...这个包含主语从句的句式，达到强调money and facilities的目的。

5. 使用强调句型

在雅思写作中，如果我们需要强调句子的某一成分（通常是主语、宾语或状语），还可以使用强调句型：**It is/was+被强调部分+that/who+原句剩余部分**。

如果强调的内容是人，引导词使用that和who均可；如果强调的内容是物，则使用that。

例1 It is *the fresh fruit* **that** tempts me at this time of year.

译1 每年这个时候吸引我的是新鲜的水果。

析1 本句强调的内容是the fresh fruit，指物，引导词只能用that。the fresh fruit为原句的主语。

例2 And it is *they* **who** will then be doing the voting.

译2 然后是他们来投票。

析2 本句强调的成分也是原句的主语，they指人，所以引导词可以用who。

例3 It is *their exports* **that** the rest of the world burns.

译3 他们的出口产品被世界其他国家所焚毁。

析3 本句强调的内容是their exports，为原句的宾语。

例4 **It is** *on that surface of the ice* **that** they have adapted ways of catching seals that are their principal prey.

译4 正是在冰面上，它们改良了捕捉海豹的方式，海豹是它们的主要猎物。

析4 本句强调的内容是地点状语，但引导词仍然要用that，不能用where。

例5 **It was** *not until railroads adopted the technology of steam* **that** they began to flourish.

译5 铁路运输采用蒸汽技术后，才开始蓬勃发展。

析5 本句强调的内容是时间状语，但引导词仍然要用that，不能用when。

同学们在雅思写作中可以借鉴和运用以上五种方式来强调观点。这些表示强调的技巧不仅可以突出重点，吸引考官和读者，还能丰富句式，展现我们的写作功力。

四 使用虚拟语气

在本书上册中，我们学习过虚拟语气。虚拟语气是说话者用来表示假设或难以实现的情况，而非客观存在事实的一种语气。此外，如需表达主观愿望或某种强烈的感情时，也可用虚拟语气。

在雅思写作中，巧妙地运用虚拟语气，不仅能使写作的句型更丰富，增强文章的语法多样性，还能使我们的语言表达更为精确和合理，为文章增色不少。

根据英语的语法，虚拟语气的结构分成许多种，可是在综合写作中，我们只需要熟悉3~4种常见的结构即可，即便是英语语法知识掌握得不那么好的考生，也可以准确使用。

1. if 引导的条件状语从句

if引导的条件状语从句可以分为两类：真实条件句和虚拟条件句。凡是假设的情况发生的可能性很大，那就是真实条件句；当假设不大可能实现时，就是虚拟条件句。if引导的条件状语从句是虚拟语气中很常见的一种结构。通常，我们通过所假设情况的发生时间来对其进行分类，可以分为虚拟现在时、虚拟过去时和虚拟将来时三类。

假设的类型	if从句谓语形式	主句谓语形式
虚拟现在时（与现在事实相反）	did/were	would/could/should/might+do
虚拟过去时（与过去事实相反）	had done	would/could/should/might+have done
虚拟将来时（与将来事实相反）	①did/were ②should do ③were to do	would/could/should/might+do

（1）虚拟现在时

在写作中，当我们要表示与现在事实相反的假设时，就可以使用虚拟现在时。虚拟现在时的基本结构是：if从句的谓语用动词的过去式（be一般用were），主句谓语用 "would/should/could/might+ 动词原形"。

例1 Such calls **would be** much more meaningful if they **were backed** by consequences for noncompliance.

译1 如果有不遵守规定的后果作为支撑，这样的呼吁将更有意义。

析1 这个句子表示与现在事实相反的假设，即 "有不遵守规定的后果作为支撑" 与现在的事实相反。因此，这句话使用虚拟现在时，if从句的谓语were backed为过去式的被动态，主句的谓语用would be。

例2 America **might sell** more cars to the islands if they **were made** with the steering wheel on the right.

译2 如果把方向盘装在右侧，美国会向这些岛屿卖出更多的车辆。

析2 这个句子表示与现在事实相反的假设，即 "把方向盘装在右侧" 与现在的事实相反。因此，这句话使用虚拟现在时，if从句的谓语were made为过去式的被动态，主句的谓语用might sell。

（2）虚拟过去时

在写作中，当我们要表示与过去事实相反的假设时，就可以使用虚拟过去时。虚拟过去时的基本结构是：if从句的谓语用过去完成时（即 "had+过去分词"），主句谓语用 "would/should/could/might+have+过去分词"。

例 If the local politicians **had been** more co-operative with the state leadership, we **would have been helped** quicker.

译 如果当时当地的政客们能与国家领导合作多一些，我们就能更快得到帮助。

析 这个句子表示与过去事实相反的假设，即当地的政客们与国家领导在过去并没有做到更好地合作。因此，这是一个虚拟过去时，if从句的谓语用过去完成时had been，主句的谓语用would have been helped。

（3）虚拟将来时

在写作中，当我们要表示与将来事实相反的假设时，就可以使用虚拟将来时。虚拟将来时的基本结构是：if从句的谓语用一般过去式(be一般用were)或用 "were to/should+动词原形"，主句谓语用 "would/should/could/might +动词原形"。

例 If you **dropped** the glass, it **would break**.

译 假如你把玻璃杯掉在地上，它会碎。

析 这是一个虚拟将来时，它表示对将来事实可能相反的假设。在此例子中，"把玻璃杯掉在地上"是一种对将来的假设，故其if从句的谓语用过去式dropped，主句的谓语用would break。

虚拟语气的倒装

当虚拟条件句的谓语部分含有 were、should、had 时，我们可以将连词 if 省略掉，而将 were、should、had 置于句首，形成部分倒装。在这类倒装结构中，置于句首的 were 习惯上不能用 was 代替。如果条件从句为否定式，注意要将 not 置于主语之后，而不置于主语之前。

例 **Should** quantitative easing be expanded, it would most likely involve the Fed buying more Treasuries and driving interest rates even lower.

译 如果扩大量化宽松政策，美联储很可能会购买更多国债，并进一步压低利率。

析 例句使用了虚拟将来时，表示对未来情况的假设。虚拟条件句 Should quantitative easing be expanded本该为 If quantitative easing should be expanded，但此句使用了倒装，should被放在句首，if被省略了。

---

2. 主语从句中的虚拟语气

虚拟语气是一个比较高级的写作手法，它的作用之一是用过去的时态表示现在或者将来的事情，表示语气弱化。因此，写作中遇到需要提建议或观点的情况，虚拟语气是一个很好的选择，比如在主语从句中使用虚拟语气。

It is/was+ 形容词/过去分词 +that+sb./sth. (should) do sth.		
常用的形容词	natural 自然的，necessary 必要的，important 重要的，possible 有可能的，advisable 可取的，desirable 值得做的	
例句	例1 **It is not necessary that** they **(should) hold** an office, and yet that is the popular idea. 译1 他们没有必要担任公职，而这是普遍的想法。 例2 **It is desirable that** interest rates **(should) be** reduced. 译2 利率下调是可取的。	
常用的过去分词	suggested 建议，ordered 命令，demanded 要求，required 需要，requested 请求，proposed 提议，advised 建议，decided 决定	
例句	例 **It is suggested that** taxes on alcohol, fuel and property **(should) rise** by 3.0%, in line with the Guernsey inflation rate for September 2012. 译 有人建议，酒税、燃油税和房产税应提高3.0%，与2012年9月根西岛的通货膨胀率保持一致。	

It is/was+ 限定词 + 名词 +that+sb./sth. (should) do sth.	
常用的名词	advice 建议, decision 决定, desire 渴望, demand 要求, idea 想法, order 命令, pity 遗憾, proposal 提议, recommendation 推荐, suggestion 建议, surprise 惊喜, wish 愿望
例句	例 **It is a crazy idea that** art students **should try** to make work and at the same time understand philosophy at that depth. 译 艺术生应努力在创作作品的同时深度理解哲学，这是个疯狂的想法。

3. 宾语从句中的虚拟语气

在表示"坚持""命令""建议""要求"之类意思的动词后的宾语从句中，要用"should+动词原形"构成的虚拟语气。其中，should 可以省略。这类宾语从句在雅思写作中很常用，可以用于表示建议和观点。

为了方便记忆，我们可以用**"一个'坚持'，两个'命令'，三个'建议'，四个'要求'"**的口诀来记住这类动词。

所用 动词	一个"坚持"	两个"命令"	三个"建议"	四个"要求"
	insist	order、command	suggest、advise、propose	ask、demand、request、require

例1 It is not unreasonable to **suggest that** Travelers **should pay** something in return for this federal subsidy.

译1 建议旅行家集团应该为这项联邦补贴支付一些费用，这不是没有道理的。

析1 在这个例子中，suggest 表示"建议（某人应该）……"，其后的宾语从句要用虚拟语气，故从句的谓语形式为"should+动词原形"，其中，should 可以省略。

例2 We should **require that** every student **be** immunized against hepatitis B.

译2 我们应该要求每一位学生都注射乙肝疫苗。

析2 在这个例子中，require 表示"要求（某人应该）……"，其后的宾语从句要用虚拟语气，此处省略了 should，故从句谓语只剩下动词原形 be。

Tips

suggest 和 insist 的两种用法

1. insist 表示"坚持认为"时，不能用虚拟语气；表示"坚持主张，坚决要求"时，用虚拟语气。例如：

例1 Fed officials continued to **insist** that the dollar **would** soon **return** to stability but disaster struck.（陈述语气）

译1 联邦政府的官员们仍坚持认为美元会很快恢复平稳，但灾难却爆发了。

例2 There are those who **insist** that we **should stop** people from speculating in the price of food.（虚拟语气）

译2 有些人坚决要求制止人们对食品价格进行投机。

2. suggest 表示"显示，表明"或"暗示"时，用陈述语气；表示"建议"时，用虚拟语气。例如：

例1 Opinion polls **suggest** that only 10% of the population **trusts** the government.（陈述语气）

译1 民意调查显示只有10%的人口信任这届政府。

例2 The architect **suggested** that the building **(should) be** restored.（虚拟语气）

译2 建筑师建议修复这座建筑。

4. 其他常见的虚拟语气句型

除了以上结构,还有一些表示虚拟语气的句型在雅思写作中很常见。

(1) would rather+从句

"would rather+从句"表示希望在现在或将来做某事或过去做过某事。would rather意为"宁愿,更喜欢"。

假设的类型	从句谓语形式	例句
与现在或将来事实相反	did/were	例Yet a poll last month found that most Americans **would rather** their government **did** less. 译然而,上个月的一项民意调查发现,大多数美国人希望他们的政府做得更少。
与过去事实相反	had done	例 I'd **rather** you **had not rung** me at work. 译我真希望你上班时没给我打电话。

(2) It is (high/about) time (that)+从句

It is (high/about) time (that)...表示"是该做……的时候了",但是实际还没有做,所以这是一种假设的情况,需要用虚拟语气。在这个句型当中,从句的谓语动词可以用过去式,也可以用"should+动词原形"的形式,其中should不可以省略。

在雅思写作中,这个句型可以用于提出倡议。

例 **It is high time** baseball umpires **did** the same during a game.

译 棒球裁判在比赛中也该这么做。

析 这个例句表示倡议,由于是倡议,所以事情肯定还没有发生,这是一种假设的情况,需要用虚拟语气。在此句中,引导词that被省略了,从句的谓语动词did使用了过去式。

五 长短句结合

如果一篇文章里全都是长难句,很可能会让读者产生视觉疲劳,令文章可读性下降,考官也可能失去耐心。而长短句结合会让你的文章错落有致,语言风格变得灵动多样,读起来更有节奏。因此,当我们的文章已经连续出现几个长句子的时候,不妨考虑替换句型,写一个短小精悍的句子。

例1 **Employees get job satisfaction in a number of ways**. Firstly, a person needs to feel that they are doing valued and valuable work, so positive feedback from superiors is very important in this respect.

译1 员工获得工作满足感的方式有很多。首先,一个人需要感觉到自己所做的工作得到重视并且有价值,所以上级的积极反馈在这方面非常重要。

析1 这是一个长短句结合的语段。在语段的开头,作者以一个简单的小短句作为总起句,引出下文的内容,而下文以长句的形式来进行分点阐述。这种长短句结合的形式,常用于"总—分"的结构,使文章主次分明,能够让读者一眼抓住重点。其次,错落有致的布局避免了读者对于长句的阅读疲劳,也增加了文章句型的多样性,值得我们借鉴。

例2 **Of course, not everyone enjoys their work**. Hard economic realities mean that many people have little choice in the kind of job they can get. In some cases, an employee is working in a job that suits neither their skills nor their personality.

译2 当然，不是每个人都喜欢自己的工作。严峻的经济现实意味着许多人对他们所能找到的工作种类几乎没有选择权。在某些情况下，员工所从事的工作既不匹配他们的技能，也不适合他们的个性。

析2 在这个例子中，作者先是用一个直白的短句简明地归纳了一种现象，而后用两个长句充分地解释了这一现象，有理有据，使人信服。这种长短句的结合形成了完整的因果论证，同时，灵活的句型变化也增加了文章的语法多样性。

小试牛刀

Exercise 1 选词填空。

1. _____ (Due to/Apart from) criminal investigation techniques, students learn forensic medicine (法医学), philosophy and logic.

2. _____ (In order to/In addition to) maximize profit, the firm would seek to maximize output.

3. _____ (Thanks to/In case of) the automobile, Americans soon had a freedom of movement previously unknown.

4. _____ (Besides/Despite) these measures, the economy remains in the doldrums (停滞).

5. _____ (Geographically/Geographical), the counties with the lowest life expectancy for women were in Appalachia and the South.

6. _____ (Suddenly/Unfortunately), there is little prospect of seeing these big questions answered.

Exercise 2 把下列句子改写成倒装句。

1. Disadvantages to the plan are there.
_____

2. Fewer tourists seem to be around there this year.
_____

3. They succeeded so well that by 2010 they were forced to reverse course. (改成 so... that 句型引导的部分倒装句)
_____

4. A taxable event occurs only when the shareholder actually sells his own shares. (改成句首为 only 引导状语的部分倒装句)
_____

5. Mothers are not only not paid, but most of their boring or difficult work is also unnoticed. (改成 not only... but (also) 结构引导的部分倒装句)
_____

Exercise 3 用横线标出下列句子中的强调部分。

1. That was the very reason why he felt a certain bitterness.

2. What matters most for the election campaign is money.

3. It is the picture itself that is the problem.

4. It was not until after the second world war that the beginnings of an explanation emerged.

5. It is they who need to start yielding—to start living and letting live.

Exercise 4 根据括号内的提示，翻译下列句子。

1. 重要的是要理解在背后影响我们行动的那些强大的经济和社会力量。(使用句型 "It+be+形容词+ to do sth.")

_____

_____

2. 很明显，父母的首要职责就是为孩子提供保护。(使用句型 "It is clear that...")

_____

_____

3. 分析师和投资者需要时间来充分消化一份报告并重新评估预期。(使用句型 "It takes+名词+(for sb.) to do sth.")

_____

_____

4. 如果他们想熬过这一关，就必须学着耐心点。(使用if虚拟条件句)

_____

_____

5. 现在是时候我们要开始理智地诚实面对这个国家所有的失败了。(使用 "It is high time+从句" 句型)

_____

_____

（答案见 pp. 125~126）

第 2 节 | 同义改写句子

在雅思写作中，为了丰富文章的语言表达，避免重复，同义改写尤为重要。同义改写的方法主要有同义词替换、同根词改写、语义概括与扩充和句型转换。

 同义词替换

同义改写最基本的一个方法是词语的同义替换。但要注意，在雅思写作中，我们不是非要选择生僻词汇或是难词才能显示出水平。我们追求的目标应该是语言的流畅、得体及地道。因此，对意思相近的雅思写作高频用词，我们应该理解并辨析其内涵及细微差别，在实际写作中，结合文章的内容、语言风格、字数篇幅等等，选用最适合的词进行写作。

以下为雅思写作中常见的同义替换词。

1. 名词类

原词	替换词	释义
human beings	mankind, human race	人类
young people	youngsters, the youth, adolescents	年轻人
old people	the old, the elderly, the aged, senior citizens	老人
teacher	instructor, educator, lecturer	老师
education	schooling, family parenting, upbringing	教育
advantage	merit, superiority, virtue	优势，优点
responsibility	obligation, duty, liability	责任
ability	capacity, power, skill	能力
entertainment	recreation, pastime, amusement	娱乐，消遣

例1 **Human beings** have great recuperative powers.

译1 人类拥有极强的恢复能力。

例2 Asia is one of the places where **mankind** originated.

译2 亚洲是人类的发源地之一。

例3 Can the **human race** carry on expanding and growing the same way that it is now?

译3 人类能够像现在这样继续发展和增长吗？

析 human beings、mankind、human race 三个词的大致意思都表示"人类"。human beings 指所有人类；mankind 可以用于表示"人类"，偶尔被用于指男性；human race 则强调人类种族。

2. 动词类

原词	替换词	释义
improve	enhance, promote, strengthen, optimize, better	提高
cause	trigger, lead to	造成，导致
solve	resolve, address, tackle, cope with, deal with	解决

destroy	impair, undermine	摧毁
develop	cultivate, foster, nurture	形成, 养成
encourage	promote, inspire, support, stimulate	鼓励, 促进
complete	fulfil, accomplish, achieve	完成
keep	preserve, retain, hold	保持
ease	alleviate, relieve, lighten	放松, 减缓

例1 Everyone can greatly **improve** the quality of life.

译1 人人都能大幅**提高**生活质量。

例2 We need to **promote** an open exchange of ideas and information.

译2 我们需要**促进**思想和信息的公开交流。

例3 Large paintings can **enhance** the feeling of space in small rooms.

译3 大幅画作能**增加**小房间的宽敞感。

例4 Figure out what kind of worker you are and manage your business to **optimize** your efforts.

译4 弄清楚你是哪一类员工, 并管理你的业务, 让你的努力得到**最大化**利用。

析 improve、promote、enhance 和 optimize 都有 "提升, 改进" 之意。其中, improve 暗含事物本身有不足之处, 需要通过改变来完善之意; promote 表示 "推广、宣传某物" 或 "提升某人职位"; enhance 则指通过提高事物的质量、特性、数量等, 让原本没有问题的事物变得更好; optimize 强调提高程度最大化。

3. 形容词类

原词	替换词	释义
good/great	conducive, beneficial, advantageous	好的, 有益的
bad	detrimental, harmful, undesirable	坏的, 不好的
poor	needy, impoverished, poverty-stricken	穷困的
obvious	apparent, evident, manifest, patent	明显的
healthy	robust, sound, wholesome	健康的
surprising	amazing, astonishing, extraordinary, miraculous	令人惊讶的
beautiful	attractive, gorgeous	美丽的, 漂亮的
energetic	dynamic, vigorous, animated, lively, vibrant	积极的, 精力充沛的
popular	prevailing, prevalent, pervasive	流行的

例1 Chairs in rows are not as **conducive** to discussion as chairs arranged in a circle.

译1 椅子成排摆放不如成圈摆放**便于讨论**。

例2 It can be **beneficial** to share your feelings with someone you trust.

译2 与你信任的人分享你的感受会是**有益的**。

例3 A free trade agreement would be **advantageous** to both countries.

译3 自由贸易协定对两国都会**有利**。

析 conducive、beneficial、advantageous 都表示 "有利的"。其中, conducive 强调环境有利于某事发生; beneficial 侧重健康、事业方面的好处; advantageous 则指有利的位置或优势令成功的机会更大。

通常来说，同义替换词只是大致词义相同，并不能达到词义的完全对等。因此，在进行同义词替换的时候，我们要注意**辨析词语的具体含义**，根据**使用情景**选择最恰当的用词。

二 同根词改写

词汇的多样性是雅思大作文评分标准的一个重要因素。在前文的基础上，我们已经积累了不少雅思写作相关用词以及同义替换词，增加了词汇量。然而，除了记忆新单词之外，在写作中，我们还可以通过同根词来丰富词汇的多样性。

以下是一些词性变化的应用例子。

例1

Some people think that more money should be spent on **promoting** the use of bicycles in cities. Others, however, believe that cities should **focus on investing** in public transport systems.	Some people argue that more money should be used in the **promotion** of the bicycle use, while others think that **the focus on** the **investment** in public transport systems is the priority in cities.

译1 一些人认为应该花更多的钱在城市里推广自行车的使用。然而，其他人认为，城市应该集中投资于公共交通系统。

析1 promote "推广，促进" 是动词，其名词形式是promotion；promoting the use of bicycles可以改写为the promotion of the bicycle use。invest "投资" 是动词，其名词形式是investment，因此investing in public transport systems可以改写为the investment in public transport systems。focus on是短语动词，可以改写为名词短语the focus on。这种做法常用来改写题目作为文章开头句。

例2

The more **flexible** primary timetable allows for more frequent, shorter sessions and for a play-centred approach; thus learners can be **enthusiastic** and **make progress**. If they are **exposed** to the language in their early childhood, they will **command** it well in later life. And learning other languages subsequently will be easier for them.	The greater **flexibility** of the primary timetable allows for more frequent, shorter sessions and for a play-centred approach, thus maintaining learners' **enthusiasm** and **progress**. Their **command** of the language in later life will benefit from this early **exposure**, while learning other languages subsequently will be easier for them.

译2 更灵活的小学课程时间表允许课程更频繁、更短，便于实行以游戏为中心的教学方法，从而能保持学习者的热情，促使其进步。长大后，他们的语言能力将从这种早期接触中受益，接下来学习其他语言对他们来说会更容易。

析2 作文中多使用名词更符合英语思维习惯，抽象和客观的表达令行文显得更正式。

例3 Instead, the traits we inherit from our parents and the situations and experiences that we encounter in life are constantly **interacting**. It is the **interaction** of the two that shapes a person's personality and dictates how that personality develops.

译3 相反，我们从父母那里继承的特质和我们在生活中的处境与经历是不断相互影响的。正是这两者的相互作用塑造了一个人的个性，并决定了个性的发展。

析3 第一句中interact作为动词说明遗传自父母的特质和生活中的经历相互作用。第二句使用了名词interaction说明正是这种相互作用慢慢地塑造了一个人的个性。作者没有用this或者it来衔接两个句子，也没有再重复一遍interacting，而是使用了interact的名词形式，并且用了强调句型It is... that，既使得衔接连贯，又增加了句式的变化。

Tips
    总而言之，我们不能忽略单词的词性变化对词汇丰富度的重要性。来尝试为你的写作用词换个词性吧，或许会有新的发现。

三 语义概括与扩充

雅思写作的语法多样性还可以通过对词语的语义进行概括与扩充来实现。

使用上义词和下义词是一种非常有效的概括与扩充语义的方法。上义词是对事物的概括性、抽象性说明；下义词指的是事物的具体表现形式。比如，colour是上义词，它的下义词是yellow、red、blue、green、purple、white等等。

1. 利用上义词

在雅思写作中，当题目出现意义比较具体的名词时，我们可以试着对此类名词进行概括总结，来实现近似于同义替换的效果。比如，在考题中看到mobile phones、televisions、computers时，我们自然可以将其总结为"电子设备""电子发明"等词，使用electronic devices、electric inventions、portable devices、electronic products等表达进行替换。如此使用上义词进行替换，有利于避免重复，增加文章用词的多样性。

例题1 **Successful sports professionals** can earn a great deal more money than people in other important professions. Some people think this is fully justified while others think it is unfair. Discuss both these views and give your own opinion.

题译1 成功的体育专业人士可以比从事其他重要职业的人赚多得多的钱。有些人认为这是完全合理的，而其他人认为这是不公平的。讨论这两种观点并给出你自己的观点。

范文1 **Celebrities such as successful sports professionals** can make much more money than people in other important occupations. Some people argue that this is fully justified while others think it is unfair.

文译1 像成功的体育专业人士这样的名人可以比从事其他重要职业的人赚更多的钱。有些人认为这是完全合理的，而其他人认为这是不公平的。

析1 在雅思写作中，对题目内容进行同义改写是书写开头段以及展开话题讨论的重要技巧。在这个例子中，要从话题展开讨论和发表观点，那么话题词successful sports professionals免不了会重复出现。由于successful sports professionals范围较小，这个时候我们可以从语义概括这方面入手，考虑使用上义词来替换，即把successful sports professionals当作下义词，寻找其符合语境的上义词，如celebrities。那么，就如范文所示，我们可以把话题词重现为Celebrities such as successful sports professionals。虽然这个新的组合仍旧有原词，但是它显示了归属关系，也展现出作者使用单词的能力，并且会显得文章的语言更丰富。

例2 Prior to the establishment of **dedicated childcare facilities**, working parents often relied on immediate family to take responsibility for the care of their children.

译2 在专门的育儿机构成立之前，双职工父母常常依靠直系亲属承担起照料孩子的重任。

例3 For parents with low incomes who are unable to afford **childcare services**, family members may indeed be their only choice for childcare.

译3 低收入的父母承担不起育儿中心的费用,依靠家庭成员也许确实是他们照顾孩子的唯一选择。

析 以上两个例句均截取自同一篇雅思真题范文。在这篇文章中,"育儿机构/中心"是题目中的话题词。在处理这个题目及下文展开论述的时候,话题词childcare facilities会不断出现。在例2中,作者使用了dedicated childcare facilities的表述,而在后文提及该话题词的时候(即例3),为了避免重复,作者使用了它的上义词childcare services("育儿服务",包含了育儿机构/中心里的服务)来进行替换。

2. 利用下义词

有时,题目中也会出现一些语义比较抽象或具有概括性的词语,如art/culture和colour/fruit/animal等,这一类词在英语中直接对应的同义替换词非常少,这时候可以利用下义词进行扩充。

对于art/culture这种抽象型的词汇,我们可以尝试把带有艺术/文化属性的具体事物列举出来进行替换,如music、paintings、architecture、traditional costumes等。对于colour/fruit/animal这种概括型的词汇,我们可以尝试把其包含的具体事物列举出来进行替换,如blue、green、yellow、red;apple、banana、watermelon;cat、tiger、dog等等。这样把话题关键词扩充成下义词,也有利于缩小写作范围,增强写作的针对性,使我们在时间有限的考场上有话可说。

例题 News reported in the media about **problems and emergencies** rather than positive developments is harmful to the individual and to society. To what extent do you agree or disagree?

题译 媒体上的新闻报道问题和紧急情况,而非积极的发展,这对个人和社会不利。你在多大程度上同意或不同意?

范文 News reported in the media about **negative events and critical situations like corruption**, **natural disasters and terrorist attacks** rather than positive developments is harmful to the individual and to society.

文译 媒体上的新闻报道负面事件和危急情况,如腐败、自然灾害、恐怖袭击等,而非积极的发展,这对个人和社会不利。

析 在这个例子中,话题词problems and emergencies的含义较宽泛,我们可以在近义词替换的基础上,寻找其下义词,对其进行扩充。problems and emergencies可以替换为negative events and critical situations,具体包括corruption、natural disasters、terrorist attacks等。扩充后,话题词的内容变得更丰富具体,有利于为我们后续写作打开思路。

Tips

除了词对词的替换外,上义词也可以用来替代句子完成同义转换。如果上文中某个句子的内容需要出现在下文,并且是作为另外一个句子的某个成分,我们可以使用以下公式:**上文内容 = 指示代词 + 上义词 = 上义词 +of this kind**。

例 In order to prepare athletes for peak performance in international competitions, more and more countries are constructing purpose-built training facilities for their local sporting talent, while ignoring the need of the general public. In my opinion, **this phenomenon** is a positive trend that gives professional athletes every possible advantage to perform at their best when representing their home country.

译 为了帮助运动员备战国际比赛，让其发挥出巅峰水平，越来越多的国家为本国的运动健儿建造专门的训练设施，而忽视了大众的需求。我认为，这是一种积极的发展方向，让职业运动员在代表祖国参赛时有尽可能多的优势赛出最佳水平。

析 第一句阐述了一种社会现象，而下一句想要继续讨论这个现象时，使用了 phenomenon 作为这个句子的上义词进行指代，简洁而连贯。在雅思写作中，像 phenomenon 这样可以概括指代上文内容的词还有 opinion、idea、behaviour、practice 等等。

四 句型的改写

在替换同义词、改变词性、概括与扩充语义的基础上，我们还可以使用同义句型进行改写。

前面介绍的倒装句、强调句等特殊句型以及被动语态、定语从句甚至是非谓语动词都是改写句子的好帮手。

除此之外，雅思写作，尤其是小作文，还会经常用到以下同义句型：

原句	同义句型
The graph shows/illustrates/represents/depicts... 该图表显示/说明/代表/描述……	The graph gives/provides information about/on... 该图表提供了关于……的信息
according to the chart/figures... 根据表格/数字……	as is shown/demonstrated/exhibited in the diagram/graph/chart/table... 如图/表所示……
over the period from... to... 在……至……期间	in the years between... and... 在……至……期间
in 1985 在1985年	in the year of 1985 在1985年
from then on 从那时起	from this time onwards 从那时起

例1 **The graph shows** how house prices have risen since the 1980s.

译1 此图表明了自20世纪80年代以来房价上涨的情况。

析1 在这个句子中，我们可以用The graph illustrates/represents/depicts... 或者 The graph gives/provides information about/on... 去替换The graph shows...。

例2 **According to the chart**, their fourth-round pick is worth 70 points, and their sixth-round pick is worth 21 points.

译2 根据图表，他们的第四轮选秀权值70分，而他们的第六轮选秀权值21分。

析2 在这个句子中，我们可以用As is shown in the chart去替换According to the chart。

例3 **Over the period from 1993 to 2011**, the largest single workforce reduction announcement by U. S. employer belongs to IBM, when it made public plans to fire 60,000 workers in July 1993.

译3 从1993年到2011年，IBM是进行单次裁员人数最多的美国雇主。1993年7月，IBM公开宣布计划解雇6万名员工。

析3 在这个句子中，我们可以用 In the years between 1993 and 2011 去替换 Over the period from 1993 to 2011。

Tips
在进行句型同义替换时，我们应该从文章字数、语言风格、语法多样性等角度出发，选择最合适的句型。

小试牛刀

Exercise 1 尽可能多地写出画线部分的同义替换词并翻译句子。

1. Young people often kick against the rules.

替换词：＿＿＿＿＿＿＿＿＿＿＿＿＿＿＿＿＿＿＿＿＿＿＿＿＿＿＿＿＿＿

翻译：＿＿＿＿＿＿＿＿＿＿＿＿＿＿＿＿＿＿＿＿＿＿＿＿＿＿＿＿＿＿＿

2. He holds strange views on education.

替换词：＿＿＿＿＿＿＿＿＿＿＿＿＿＿＿＿＿＿＿＿＿＿＿＿＿＿＿＿＿＿

翻译：＿＿＿＿＿＿＿＿＿＿＿＿＿＿＿＿＿＿＿＿＿＿＿＿＿＿＿＿＿＿＿

3. A small car has the added advantage of being cheaper to run.

替换词：＿＿＿＿＿＿＿＿＿＿＿＿＿＿＿＿＿＿＿＿＿＿＿＿＿＿＿＿＿＿

翻译：＿＿＿＿＿＿＿＿＿＿＿＿＿＿＿＿＿＿＿＿＿＿＿＿＿＿＿＿＿＿＿

4. Eating out is the national pastime in France.

替换词：＿＿＿＿＿＿＿＿＿＿＿＿＿＿＿＿＿＿＿＿＿＿＿＿＿＿＿＿＿＿

翻译：＿＿＿＿＿＿＿＿＿＿＿＿＿＿＿＿＿＿＿＿＿＿＿＿＿＿＿＿＿＿＿

5. They can be trusted to solve major national problems.

替换词：＿＿＿＿＿＿＿＿＿＿＿＿＿＿＿＿＿＿＿＿＿＿＿＿＿＿＿＿＿＿

翻译：＿＿＿＿＿＿＿＿＿＿＿＿＿＿＿＿＿＿＿＿＿＿＿＿＿＿＿＿＿＿＿

6. You should encourage your child's attempts at self-expression.

替换词：＿＿＿＿＿＿＿＿＿＿＿＿＿＿＿＿＿＿＿＿＿＿＿＿＿＿＿＿＿＿

翻译：＿＿＿＿＿＿＿＿＿＿＿＿＿＿＿＿＿＿＿＿＿＿＿＿＿＿＿＿＿＿＿

7. It is not surprising that children learn to read at different rates.

替换词：＿＿＿＿＿＿＿＿＿＿＿＿＿＿＿＿＿＿＿＿＿＿＿＿＿＿＿＿＿＿

翻译：＿＿＿＿＿＿＿＿＿＿＿＿＿＿＿＿＿＿＿＿＿＿＿＿＿＿＿＿＿＿＿

8. This is an opportunity to enhance the reputation of the company.

替换词：＿＿＿＿＿＿＿＿＿＿＿＿＿＿＿＿＿＿＿＿＿＿＿＿＿＿＿＿＿＿

翻译：＿＿＿＿＿＿＿＿＿＿＿＿＿＿＿＿＿＿＿＿＿＿＿＿＿＿＿＿＿＿＿

9. Governments should adopt a more proactive approach to eliminating preventable illnesses and diseases by addressing associated pollution and housing problems.

替换词：＿＿＿＿＿＿＿＿＿＿＿＿＿＿＿＿＿＿＿＿＿＿＿＿＿＿＿＿＿＿

翻译：＿＿＿＿＿＿＿＿＿＿＿＿＿＿＿＿＿＿＿＿＿＿＿＿＿＿＿＿＿＿＿

10. Many people blame <u>excessive</u> violence in television programs and movies for the increasing rate of violent crimes, and therefore government censorship of such media content should be imposed.

替换词: _____

翻译: _____

Exercise 2　用括号内单词的正确形式填空。

1. The _____ (invent) has been patented by the university.

2. There is a growing _____ (realise) that changes must be made.

3. Computers offer a much greater degree of _____ (flexible) in the way work is organised.

4. The department denies _____ (responsible) for what occurred.

5. There has already been a definite _____ (improve).

6. _____ (priority) to distribution in Chinese theatres, all screenplays in China must be approved by SARFT (国家广播电视总局).

7. As the problem of environmental destruction becomes more _____ (evidence) and widely known, individuals everywhere are doing their part to save the earth.

Exercise 3　根据提示，对画线部分进行同义改写。

1. <u>According to the table</u>, American workers have very good reason to be afraid. (使用同义句型)

_____

_____

2. People believe that using <u>mobile phones and computers</u> to communicate makes us lose the ability to communicate with each other face to face. (使用上义词)

_____

_____

3. The government should control the amount of <u>violence in films and on television</u> in order to decrease violent crimes in society. (使用上义词)

_____

_____

4. Many <u>customs and traditional ways of behaviour</u> are no longer relevant to the modern life and not worth keeping. (使用下义词)

_____

_____

5. Some people think that <u>environmental problems</u> are too big for individuals to solve. Others, however, believe that the problems cannot be solved if individuals do not take actions. (使用下义词)

_____

_____

（答案见 pp. 126~127）

第3节 常用的论证句型

在雅思写作中，对主要观点进行论证时，常用的句型有三种：因果句、假设句和比较句。应用好这些论证句型可以使得观点的阐述更充实，更具有说服力。

一 因果句的写法

在雅思写作中，因果句可以帮助我们引入支撑观点的理由和例证。它揭示了事物之间普遍存在的因果关系，使论证过程更具有逻辑性。

顾名思义，因果句，有原因有结果。A 导致 B 的发生，那么 A 就是原因，B 就是结果。

在写因果句的时候要注意句子的逻辑，明确哪一部分是原因，哪一部分是结果。

1. 因果句写作实例

例 ① Cognitive development plays a major role in determining a person's ability to judge right from wrong. ② Adolescents are still developing their mental faculties, and they do not have the same level of cognitive function and reasoning capacity as adults. ③**For this reason**, when young people commit serious crimes, they may be incapable of fully understanding the implications of their actions before, during, or even after the fact.

译 ①认知发展在培养一个人判断是非的能力上起着主要的作用。②青少年的心智尚在发育，他们的认知水平和推理能力并不如成年人。③**因此**，青少年在犯下严重罪行时，可能在事前、事中甚至事后都无法充分理解其行为的后果。

析 这篇范文的主题是少年犯应否与成人同罚。范文的中心论点是在法律面前儿童和成年人并不等同，在对罪犯量刑时应考虑年龄问题。在这一段落中，句①指出认知发展对是非判断力的重要性，句②进一步指出青少年的心智尚未发展成熟，句③用 For this reason 连接上下文，指出心智仍在发展导致的结果是青少年在犯罪时未能充分意识其行为带来的后果。句①②是层层递进的原因，句③阐述其结果。这是典型的因果论证。

2. 因果句的表达方式

（1）因果句的语序

因果句的语序有两种：一是先写原因后写结果，二是先写结果后写原因。

- **先写原因，后写结果**

例 It encourages use of private cars and **therefore** worsens traffic congestion and greenhouse emissions.

译 这种做法鼓励使用私家车，因此会加剧交通拥堵和温室气体排放。

析 在这个句子中，therefore 是副词，意为"所以"。It encourages use of private cars 表示原因，导致的结果是 (It) worsens traffic congestion and greenhouse emissions。

- **先写结果，后写原因**

例 People are living to a very old age **because** medical care is improving.

译 因为医疗服务越发完善，所以现在人们的寿命很长。

析 在这个句子中，because 是连词，意为"因为"。它将两个分句连接在一起，引出原因。People are living to a very old age 是结果，medical care is improving 是原因。

因果句的两种语序可以相互转换,将"先原因后结果"转换为"先结果后原因",或反之亦然。比如,上面的两个例句可以进行如下的转换:

例1 It encourages use of private cars and **therefore** worsens traffic congestion and greenhouse emissions.

→It worsens traffic congestion and greenhouse emissions **because** it encourages use of private cars.

例2 People are living to a very old age **because** medical care is improving.

→Medical care is improving, **so** people are living to a very old age.

(2)表达因果关系的短语和句型

在写因果句时,我们可以用不同的短语和句型来表达因果关系。下列表格分别列出了引导原因和结果的常用表达。

● 引出原因

类别	用语	例句
连词(后接分句)	because/since/as/for 因为	例 And the machine wouldn't be able to explain why its treatment was plausible **because** its machine-learning algorithms were simply too complex to be fully understood by humans. 译 机器无法解释为什么它的治疗方案是合理的,因为它的机器学习算法太复杂了,人类无法完全理解。
短语介词(后接名词)	owing to/due to/ thanks to/because of/ as a result of 因为,由于	例 In some countries, an increasing number of people are suffering from health problems **as a result of** eating too much fast food. 译 在一些国家,越来越多的人因为吃了太多快餐而受到健康问题的困扰。
句型	the reason for/ the cause of sth. is (that)... 某事的原因是……	例 He thinks **the reason for** the lack of comments **is that** potential reviewers lack incentive. 译 他认为没有评论的原因是潜在的审查者缺乏动力。

● 引出结果

类别	用语	例句
连词或连接副词	so (that)/accordingly/ consequently/hence/ therefore/thus 所以,因此	例 If fewer young people are moving into teaching as a profession, there could be several reasons for this trend and **hence** several ways to encourage them into it. 译 如果越来越少的年轻人进入教师这个行业,可能有几个原因造成这种趋势,因此也有几种方法来鼓励他们进入这个行业。

动词(后接名词)	result in/lead to/ give rise to/cause 导致,造成	例 Having to deal with this persistent linguistic competition can **result in** difficulties, however. 译 然而,不得不处理这种持续的语言竞争会带来很多困难。
介词短语	as a result/ as a consequence/ for this reason/ for these reasons 所以,因此	例 **As a result**, there is considerable variation throughout the world in the roles that mothers and fathers adopt. 译 因此,在全球各地,父亲和母亲承担的角色有相当大的差异。
句型	... is the cause of sth. ……导致某事	例 Smartphones can also, however, **be the cause of** social or medical problems. 译 然而,智能手机也可能导致社会或医疗问题。

Tips

1. 注意区分result in和result from:result in+结果;result from+原因。

2. 注意区分as a result和as a result of:as a result+结果;as a result of+原因。

3. cause既可以作名词也可以作动词:作名词时意为"原因";作动词时意为"导致,引起",后面跟结果。

试比较:

例1 This **causes** an inability to focus on anything, which makes time seem to go painfully slowly.

译1 这导致我们无法专注于任何事情,使得时间似乎过得很慢,令人痛苦。

析1 在这个例句中,cause是动词,表示"导致,引起",后面的内容为结果。

例2 It is unlikely that there was a single **cause** for the decline of the civilisation.

译2 这个文明衰落的原因不大可能只有一个。

析2 在这个例句中,cause是名词,表示"原因"。

二 假设句的写法

　　假设句是假定一种情况,推测在这一情况下可能产生的结果。假设论证是运用假设推理对论据进行分析的过程,可以使得论证更加充分。在雅思写作中,我们经常需要扩展观点,而扩展观点的一种常用方法就是做假设,在举例子时尤其有用。

1. 假设句写作实例

例 ①As the global population rises, so does the demand for consumer goods, which can lead to an increase in the rate of environmental devastation. ②Consumer goods that are non-biodegradable, such as plastic, glass, metal products, and electronic devices, do not break down naturally over time. ③Non-biodegradables can cause significant damage to the environment **if** they end up in landfill or other areas not designated for their disposal.

译 ①随着全球人口数量增长,消费品的需求量也在增长,这会导致环境破坏的速度加快。②不可生物降解的消费品如塑料、玻璃、金属制品以及电子设备,不会随着时间的推移而自然降解。③这些产品若是最后被丢到了垃圾填埋场或指定处理地点以外的其他地方,就会对环境造成重大危害。

析 这篇范文的主题是消费品产量增长破坏自然环境。在这一段落中，句①是主题句，指出消费品需求的增长可能导致环境更快被破坏。句②和句③是对这一主题句，即这一段的中心观点进行扩展和论述。句②指出，不可生物降解的消费品不会自然降解；句③进行假设，如果这些消费品处理不当，就会对环境造成重大危害。句③通过做假设，能够更好地对观点进行扩展论述，使论述更加全面。

2. 使用条件状语从句做假设

在写作中进行假设论证时，往往用到条件状语从句。条件状语从句的引导词有 if、unless、provided that、on condition that 等。

引导词	例句
if 如果	例 **If** people are granted unrestrained access to fresh water supplies, the risk of excessive and disproportionate consumption is virtually a certainty. 译 如果人们可以不受限制地获得淡水供应，那么几乎必然存在过度消耗和不成比例的消耗的风险。
unless 除非（相当于if not）	例 We cannot understand disease **unless** we understand the person who has the disease. 译 除非我们了解患有某种疾病的人，否则我们不会了解该疾病。
on condition that 在……的条件下	例 She would only accept the position **on condition that** she was given the contract in writing. 译 只有收到了书面合同，她才会接受这份工作。
provided (that) 如果，只要	例 The Internet is an invaluable resource for students of all ages, **provided that** it is used sensibly. 译 只要合理利用，互联网对各年龄段的学生而言都是宝贵的资源。
as long as/ so long as 只要	例 People have the right to choose how they live, **as long as** they do not place themselves or others in danger. 译 人们有权选择生活的方式，只要他们不将自己或他人置于危险之中。

三 比较句的写法

在雅思写作中，使用比较句能够直观地突出差异或进行类比。

1. 比较句写作实例

例 ① Older people are ideal for managerial positions for a number of reasons. ② First and foremost, it generally takes many years of hard work and dedication to be promoted to the most senior positions within a company. ③ Therefore, by the time an employee is ready to take on a top-level management role, he will have acquired a wealth of knowledge and experience that allow him to successfully lead a team of subordinates. ④ Young people, on the other hand, **are** invariably **less experienced** and yet to gain the necessary knowledge required for being a company leader.

译 ①年龄更大的人是管理职位的理想人选，理由有很多。②最重要的一点是，要晋升到一个企业最高级的职位通常需要多年的努力工作和奉献。③因此，到一名员工合适担任高级的管理职位时，他已经有足够的知识和经验，可以成功带领团队，领导下属。④而年轻人则难免经验不足，尚未学到作为企业领导所必须具备的知识。

析 这篇范文的主题是年轻人是否适合当领导。范文的中心论点是年龄更大的人是企业高管层的最佳人选。这一段落陈述了支撑观点的主要原因。句①是承上启下句，句②说明当领导通常需要多年的努力和奉献，句③具体说明老员工有足够的知识和经验，句④使用比较论证，将年轻人与老员工进行对比突出了老员工当领导的优势。

2. 比较句的基本结构

雅思写作中常用的比较句包括同级比较和比较级比较两种基本结构。

（1）同级比较：as+ 形容词 / 副词原级 +as

例 With new media, we all want the world to change **as fast as** our technology does.

译 有了新媒体，我们都希望世界变化与我们的技术变化一样快。

（2）比较级比较：形容词 / 副词比较级 +than

例 Children learn **faster than** adults.

译 孩子比大人学得快。

在 as... as 结构中，第一个 as 是副词，修饰其后的形容词或副词；而第二个 as 是连词，后可接名词或从句。而在 than 结构中，than 也是连词。因此，这两种类型的比较句本质是一致的。连词 as 或 than 后的部分会运用**省略、倒装、替代**等手段。

3. 比较句中的省略、倒装和替代

（1）比较句中的省略

比较句中重复的部分可以适当省略，让句子结构更简洁，突出比较的重点。

例 The cello is **lower than** the violin.

译 大提琴的声音比小提琴低沉。

析 我们可以将这个比较句拆分为两个独立分句：

The violin is low. + The cello is lower.

→The cello is lower than the violin is.

→The cello is lower than the violin.

上面的句子中，low 和 is 是重复的，所以最后都省略删去了。

Tips

比较从句中的谓语动词省略后可能会产生歧义，这时不可直接省略，需要使用 do、have 的适当时态形式或相应情态动词替换。

例 Our brains need a rest **as much as** our bodies **do**.

译 我们的大脑和我们的身体一样需要休息。

析 我们可以将这个比较句拆分为两个独立分句：

Our bodies need a rest.

Our brains need a rest as much.

如果我们将以上两个句子用 as... as 的同级比较结构合并起来的话，可以写成：

Our brains need a rest as much as our bodies need a rest.

若直接将这句话重复的部分都删掉，则句子简化为：

Our brains need a rest as much as our bodies.

此时，这句话产生了歧义：句中的 our bodies 是作主语（与 Our brains 比较），还是作宾语（与 a rest 比较）？即这句话可理解为"我们的大脑和我们的身体一样需要休息"或"我们的大脑就像需要身体一样需要休息"。为了避免歧义，例句没有直接省略从句的谓语动词，而是用 do 替代。

（2）比较句中的倒装

若比较从句中的谓语动词为 do、have 或相应情态动词所替换，那么从句可以使用倒装结构。

例 A single full-size cigar contains **as much** nicotine **as** *do* several cigarettes.

译 单根足尺寸的雪茄中含有的尼古丁相当于好几根香烟中尼古丁的含量。

析 这个比较句可以看作是两个句子的合并：

Several cigarettes contain much nicotine.

+A single full-size cigar contains as much nicotine.

→A single full-size cigar contains as much nicotine as several cigarettes *do*. (do在这里指代重复的谓语动词contain)

→A single full-size cigar contains as much nicotine as *do* several cigarettes. （将比较从句中的谓语动词进行倒装）

一般情况下，当从句的主语是名词短语且较长时就采用倒装结构，而主语是代词时一般不倒装。我们通过以下两个例句进行理解：

例1 Komatiites are Earth's oldest known volcanic rocks and contain **three times as much** magnesium **as** *do* most volcanic rocks.

译1 科马提岩是地球上已知的最古老的火山岩，含镁量是大多数火山岩的三倍。

析1 three times as much... as是表达倍数的比较句，从句的主语most volcanic rocks是名词短语且较长，故用倒装结构。

例2 People stare at paragraphs **longer than** they *do* at images.

译2 人们看文本段落的时间要多于看图像的时间。

析2 例句中的 than they do at images 相当于 than they stare at images，从句的主语是人称代词they，故不使用倒装。

（3）比较句中的替代

在比较句中可使用代词 that 或 those 进行替代，避免重复。

例1 The timbre of the violin is far **richer than** *that* of the mouth organ.

译1 小提琴的音色比口琴的音色丰富得多。

析1 例句将小提琴的音色与口琴的音色进行比较,该句子本来是"The timbre of the violin is far richer than the timbre of the mouth organ.",但由于英语不喜重复,故用代词that替代前面出现过的The timbre。注意,替代单数名词用that,替代复数名词用those。

例2 In firms in general, the average hourly wages of part-timers are **lower than** *those* of full-timers.

译2 一般来说，在公司中，兼职人员的平均时薪低于全职员工的平均时薪。

析2 例句将兼职人员的平均时薪与全职员工的平均时薪进行比较。those替代的是前面出现过的the average hourly wages。

除了代词，还可使用名词counterpart(s)来进行替代。

counterpart(s)表示"对应的事物，职位(作用)相当的人或物"，在比较句中，本质上是替代词。

例3 Some evidence suggests that household heads with college or postgraduate degrees were paying a **higher** price on onions, peppers and potatoes **than** their *counterparts*.

译3 一些证据表明，拥有大学或研究生学位的家庭户主在洋葱、辣椒和土豆上支付的价格高于其他家庭户主。

析3 此比较句将拥有大学或研究生学位的家庭户主与没有大学或研究生学位的家庭户主进行比较。例句中的their counterparts指的是other household heads without college or postgraduate degrees。

Tips

在比较句写作中，比较的对象需要保持一致，即前后比较的事物要一致。比较句写作中常见错误如下：

例 The timbre of the violin is far richer than the mouth organ. ✗

The timbre of the violin is far richer than **the timbre of** the mouth organ. ✓

The timbre of the violin is far richer than **that of** the mouth organ. ✓

译 小提琴的音色比口琴的音色丰富得多。

这个比较句比较的是"小提琴的音色"和"口琴的音色"，即不同乐器音色的比较。错句中将"小提琴的音色"（音色）和"口琴"（乐器）相比较，比较的事物不一致，所以是不对的。从句中需要补全the timbre of，意思才正确，但由于英语不喜重复，所以可以用代词that替代。

4. 表达比较的句型

比较级	例 Their objective is to make AI technologies **more trustworthy and transparent**, so that organisations and individuals understand how AI decisions are made. 译 他们的目标是使人工智能技术变得更加可信和透明，以便组织和个人了解人工智能的决策是如何做出的。
比较级+than	例 Surprisingly, the bilinguals' brains had **more** physical signs of disease **than** their monolingual counterparts, even though their outward behaviour and abilities were the same. 译 令人惊讶的是，双语者的大脑比单语者的大脑有更多的疾病体征，即使他们的外在行为和能力是相同的。
as... as **(否定形式：not** **as/so... as)**	例1 If the sales figures are **as bad as** predicted, the company will probably go bankrupt. 译1 如果销售数据像预测的那样糟糕，公司可能会破产。 例2 The available pool of healthy manpower was **not as large as** military officials had expected. 译2 一拨可用的健康劳力人数达不到军方官员们的期望值。

as many/much as+ 可数名词复数	例1 She gets **as many as** eight thousand letters a month.
	译1 她每月收到多达8,000封信。
	例2 Some old machines go for **as much as** 35,000 dollars.
	译2 一些旧机器以高达3.5万美元的价格出售。
	析2 as much as用于修饰金额、距离、时间等不可数概念,但后面接的仍可能是可数名词复数。此句中, dollars是可数名词复数,但35,000 dollars这个金额是不可数的概念,故用as much as。
more of a/an+名词+than	例 Running an efficient IT organisation is much **more of a** science **than** an art.
	译 运营一个高效的信息技术组织更像是一门科学,而不是一门艺术。
as much of a/an+名词+as	例 Santa races are becoming **as much of a** tradition **as** candy canes and Christmas lights.
	译 圣诞老人比赛正在成为与糖果手杖和圣诞灯一样的传统。
倍数+as+形容词/副词原级+as	例 She earns **five times as much as** I do.
	译 她挣的钱是我挣的五倍。
倍数+as many+可数名词复数+as 倍数+as much+不可数名词+as	例1 New drivers have **twice as many accidents as** experienced drivers.
	译1 新手司机所出的事故是老司机的两倍。
	例2 Mothers today spend about **twice as much time** with their kids **as** fathers do.
	译2 如今母亲花在孩子身上的时间大约是父亲花的两倍。
倍数+形容词/副词比较级+than	例 Some people think that online shopping is **ten times better than** going to a shopping centre.
	译 有些人认为,网上购物比去购物中心购物好十倍。
倍数+the size/ height/length/ width etc.+of	例 But married couples earn on average **three times the incomes of** single people.
	译 但已婚夫妇的平均收入是单身人士的三倍。

Tips

在写比较句时,我们可以在比较级前使用副词进行修饰,常用的副词修饰语有 much、far、a great deal、a lot、a little、a bit、slightly 等。如:

例 Employees subscribed for *far more* shares **than** were available.

译 雇员们申购了远比实际数额还多的股份。

✎ 小试牛刀

Exercise 1 选词填空。

1. Many people cannot afford to buy their own house _____ (due to/resulting in) the housing shortage.

2. Their bodies had suffered contortion _____ (leading to/as a result of) malnutrition.

3. A passive, boring activity is best for creativity _____ (because/therefore) it allows the mind to wander.

4. A colder turn in the Scandinavian climate would likely have meant widespread crop failures, _____ (because/so) more people would have depended on hunting to make up for those losses.

5. Out in the wild, the ants probably don't live for a full 140 days _____ (thanks to/leading to) predators, disease and just being in an environment that's much harsher than the comforts of the lab.

6. He needs more time _____ (owing to/causing) the special circumstances of the Great Recession.

7. Vehicles with limited self-driving capabilities have been around for more than 50 years, _____ (resulting from/resulting in) significant contributions towards driver assistance systems.

8. We suspect they are trying to hide something, _____ (since/hence) the need for an independent inquiry.

9. The universities have expanded, _____ (as/thus) allowing many more people the chance of higher education.

10. First, there is a lack of information flow, and _____ (due to/consequently) degradation in the quality of advice.

Exercise 2 用 if 或 unless 合并句子。

例 We know what's going to happen next. Then we don't get excited.
  →*If* we know what's going to happen next, then we don't get excited.

1. We want AI to really benefit people.
  We need to find a way to get people to trust it.
  _____

2. Students are not allowed to handle these chemicals.
  They are under the supervision of a teacher.
  _____

3. Mobility demand can be met by far fewer vehicles.
  A significant proportion of the population choose to use shared automated vehicles.
  _____

4. Individuals cannot solve these environmental problems.
  Governments take some actions.
  _____

5. It is impossible for children to succeed at school.
  They have help from their parents.
  _____

Exercise 3 改正下列句子中的错误。

1. NPR's audience tends to be more wide-ranging than other music sites.

2. Human children depend on adults for much longer than any other primate (灵长类动物).

3. Many decisions in our lives require a good forecast, and AI is almost always good at forecasting than we are.

4. He takes us into the world of microbes in a bid to persuade us to love them as more as he does.

5. Since his injury, Jones has become much of a liability than an asset to the team.

Exercise 4　根据括号内的提示词，翻译下列句子。

1. 无人驾驶汽车的引入将带来更高的安全性。(result in)

_____

_____

2. 回收利用也减少了对原材料开采(quarry)的需求，从而节省了宝贵的资源。(thus)

_____

_____

3. 出于这个原因，在需要处理冲突的任务上，双语人士往往表现得更好。(for this reason)

_____

_____

4. 这有数百个频道，因此你总能找到值得一看的东西。(therefore)

_____

_____

5. 如果土壤失去了执行(perform)这些功能的能力，人类可能会遇到大麻烦。(if)

_____

_____

6. 他同意在不暴露身份的条件下和记者谈话。(on condition that)

_____

_____

7. 除非创造更多工作机会，否则复苏(recovery)无法保持下去。(unless)

_____

_____

8. 猫睡觉的时间是人的两倍。(倍数+as... as)

_____

_____

9. 许多笼中鸟比野外同类鸟的寿命长。(比较级+than)

_____

_____

10. 埃博拉病毒(Ebola)不像天花(smallpox)这类病毒那样容易传播。(not as... as)

_____

_____

（答案见 pp. 127~129）

第 <big>4</big> 章　写作综合训练 250 句

第 1 节　基础训练 150 句

Exercise 1　改正句子中的错误。

1. Each of us have a role to play in promoting equality and social justice in our communities.

2. In the 18th century, art along with music and poetry, were seen as something edifying (启迪的).

3. These exercises aim counteract the effects of stress and tension.

4. Read this essay was an elevating (有启发的) experience.

5. In fact, many people will go to great lengths to save time and avoid to expend this precious commodity.

6. It is not uncommon for college students having bank loans.

7. It was as if the animals did not know how coping with their newfound freedom.

8. People love this tool because they can participate in a town hall meeting without to leave their home.

9. News travel fast these days.

10. Critics and the public puzzle out the layers of meaning in his photoes.

11. The informations were not easily classifiable.

12. This recent discoveries show that plenty of goods travelled on overland routes.

13. This new research adds a few more evidence to help decide where the balance should lie.

14. Another solutions may be to reveal more about the algorithms which AI uses and the purposes they serve.

15. We have been running the programme since ten years and we don't like to change the basic technology.

16. Courses range from cooking in computing.

17. All endeavours strive with balance, harmony and unity with nature and one another.

18. The classic problem is whether central banks can credibly commit in maintaining inflation once recovery appears to be under way.

19. Parking lot owners should be legally responsible in protecting vehicles.

20. The club could be deducted 10 points as a result from this move.

21. Although they're expensive, but they last forever and never go out of style.

22. Sightseeing is best done either by tour bus and by bicycle.

23. Five years ago neither entrepreneurship or technology was as cool or in demand as it is today.

24. Because it is the language of the Internet and e-commerce, so English has become the international language.

25. Scientists have looked at some similar aspects in bees, so the results of recent bee studies are mixed.

26. As technology becomes increasing complex, finding those greater depths in computer art could become possible.

27. Overall, the oil price has increased sharp due to a diminishing supply and a rising demand.

28. Admitted, shale (页岩) is responsible for a fifth of the 18.3% increase in overall industrial production.

29. All of these are useful breeds which potentiality has not been realized.

30. Some people say we have reached the point which technology is intruding on our private lives.

31. Other studies show that keeping a dog as a pet gives children early exposure to a diverse range of bacteria, that may help protect them against allergies later.

32. A number of crimes such as identity theft result from the ease in which criminals can operate anonymously online.

33. Anything which makes it easier for suppliers to share their designs will save time and money.

34. People are rewarded for that they accomplish, if given equal opportunity.

35. How they do offer is a good product at a rock-bottom price.

36. One essential question is if the bank's role would go beyond monitoring to providing financial assistance.

37. Indeed, countless victims have been such severely affected by crime that they believe crime prevention is a lost cause.

38. Housing prices are such high that most people can't afford to live anywhere near the coast.

39. The disk will corrupt if it will be overloaded.

40. In the future, computers will use to create bigger and even more sophisticated computers.

41. The two maps illustrate the changes that were taken place in a museum and its surrounding areas between 1990 and 2010.

42. Only when wider social problems, such as poverty and inequality, are eliminated, crime will disappear.

43. No sooner the video was up than thousands of people across the world wanted to see.

44. It is only the achievement of these goals which will finally bring lasting peace.

45. Local people demanded that the police apprehended (逮捕) the miscreants (歹徒).

46. It is time that those who have created the crisis pay for it.

47. Competition can be healthy, but if it is pushed too far it can result from bullying.

48. The digital economy is growing seven times fast than the rest of the economy.

49. Densely packed pedestrian traffic loads can weigh more than that of passenger cars.

50. The road to the sunny, clean future is not as smoother as it seemed.

Exercise 2 按照提示，合并句子。

1. I think universities should provide theoretical knowledge. I think universities should incorporate practical skills into the curriculum. (用连词and合并)

_____

_____

2. Transportation is estimated to account for 30% of energy consumption in most of the world's most developed nations. Lowering the need for energy-using vehicles is essential for decreasing the environmental impact of mobility. (用连词so合并)

_____

_____

3. We might associate wisdom with intelligence or particular personality traits. Research shows only a small positive relationship between wise thinking and crystallised intelligence and the personality traits of openness and agreeableness. (用连词 but 合并)

_____

_____

4. The awareness of competition could also serve as a positive factor in enhancing personal skills. These personal skills include time management and communication. (用 such as 合并)

_____

_____

5. I insist that teachers take on a very important role in education. It should not be ignored. (用 so … that 合并)

_____

_____

6. The product was a hit. Women wore them as accessories around concert grounds. (用 such… that 合并)

_____

_____

7. Certain aspects of parenting may come naturally. I agree that taking a parenting course can benefit both parents and children. (用 although 合并)

_____

_____

8. We possess both the science and the technology to identify and redress the changes in how we read. Otherwise, the changes become entrenched (根深蒂固的).(用 before 合并)

_____

_____

9. An individual saw an advertisement for Big Macs on television earlier that day. He might go to McDonald's and purchase five Big Mac burgers. (用 after 合并)

_____

_____

10. Laws may be needed to boost the amount of recycling. I believe that educating residents is much more important and a better way to achieve the same outcome. (用 while 合并)

_____

_____

11. Far-reaching reforms are not implemented. The economy is in danger of collapse. (用 unless 合并)

_____

_____

12. Actually, art classes provide a distraction. They allow our students a break from their intense study and constant competition.(用现在分词合并)

_____

_____

13. Another disadvantage of always trying to outstrip（超越）others is mental problems. The mental problems result from constant pressure.(用现在分词合并)

_____

_____

14. We see the towering buildings from afar. They beckon（召唤）the visitor in.(用过去分词合并)

_____

_____

15. William Janssen travelled around Thailand in the 1990s. He was impressed with the basic rooftop solar heating systems that were on many homes.(用现在分词合并)

_____

_____

16. We had learned a lesson. We reacted.(用现在分词的完成式合并)

_____

_____

17. Dads talked to kids. Dads didn't raise their pitch or fundamental frequency.(用when合并)

_____

_____

18. We should adapt ourselves to it. We shouldn't prevent it.(用rather than合并)

_____

_____

19. The fear of losing job security is often strong. It essentially paralyses people to the point of settling for mediocrity（平庸）and never venturing outside of their comfort zone.(用so… that合并)

_____

_____

20. Almost all agencies have the same basic capabilities. Their creative standards differ.(用despite the fact that合并)

_____

_____

21. Children's bodies are ready. Then they learn to walk.(用not… until合并)

_____

_____

22. There were around 550,000 visitors in the Natural History Museum. 400,000 visitors went to the Science Museum.(用whereas合并)

_____

_____

23. Theoretical knowledge prepares us for further education. This is essential since lifelong learning is more necessary than ever in this ever-evolving society.(用定语从句合并)

_____

_____

24. Some young children have not yet commenced their primary school education. Childcare centres exist to ensure the safety and well-being of these young children. (用定语从句合并)

_____

_____

25. People are depressed. People eat.(用when合并)

_____

_____

26. Needless to say, this necessitates a long-term commitment to countless hours of hard work. This kind of commitment requires steadfast determination.(用定语从句合并)

_____

_____

27. Two different goods have the same price. It can be claimed that they produce the same quantity of pleasure in the consumer. (用if合并)

_____

_____

28. As global temperatures continue to rise, we are going to continue to squander (浪费) more and more energy on keeping our buildings mechanically cool. We have run out of capacity. (用until合并)

_____

_____

29. Art and music are historically traditional to the country. A government wants to preserve and maintain the art and music. It must take steps to ensure that those traditions are valued and fostered. (用if和定语从句合并)

_____

_____

30. Here I am referring to the print newspaper. Its readership is indeed steadily declining in the past decade.(用定语从句合并)

_____

_____

31. People travel on the underground. They don't carry their bikes around. (用定语从句合并)

_____

_____

32. Older parents generally have less stressed about income or job security. They tend to be more patient and can spend more time with their children.(用 so that 合并)

_____

_____

33. The culture remains intact. The team will eventually find its success.(用 as long as 合并)

_____

_____

34. Our stories were not the same. I found myself in each one of them.(用 yet 合并)

_____

_____

35. Women are looking for career development. Women are making a contribution to the nation.(用 as well as 合并)

_____

_____

36. Access to information and knowledge is much easier today than in the past. I still insist that teachers take on a role so important in education that it should not be ignored.(用 even if 合并)

_____

_____

37. This is an important step to ensure what is learned is useful. This is also an important step to prevent students from accessing information that would produce deleterious effects on their mentality.(用 not only... but also 合并)

_____

_____

38. The website was set up to allow individuals to create itineraries and travel packages to suit their own needs and interests. The website was also set up to allow travel organisations to do the same thing. (用 both... and 合并)

_____

_____

39. You can try to dance to it. You can try to escape it as much as possible. (用 either... or 合并)

_____

_____

40. The majority of workers work unofficially with no health insurance. They have no wage security either. (用 neither... nor 合并)

_____

41. There are more durable materials. Today's editions are likely to survive in large quantities. (用 thanks to 合并)

_____

42. It is a very hopeful principle when applied to critical thought in the reading brain. It implies choice. (用 because 合并)

_____

43. Some workers were later allowed back in. The other workers were told to return by the factory owners. (用 or 合并)

_____

44. This mindset takes over. The potential for neglect, abuse, and even destruction of the local culture and environment will increase dramatically.(用 as soon as 合并)

_____

45. They want to come to the clinic. They can come to the clinic. (用 whenever 合并)

_____

46. The project is completed. Performances will increase, and museum opening hours will be extended.(用 once 合并)

_____

47. There is such demand for tropical agribusiness in an area. Forests in that area are being razed (彻底摧毁) to meet it. (用 wherever 合并)

_____

48. The laws came into effect. Their movements have been severely circumscribed (限制).(用 since 合并)

_____

49. These advancements continue to be informed by our collective humanity and desire for progress. The outlook is promising. (用 provided that 合并)

_____

_____

50. Children reach the age of 15. This figure almost doubles to 18%.(用 by the time 合并)

_____

_____

Exercise 3 按照提示，改写句子。

1. In the business world, company directors and managers are commonly older than other employees. (It+ be+形容词+for sb. to do sth.)

_____

_____

2. Generally, to be promoted to the most senior positions within a company needs many years of hard work and dedication.(It takes… to do sth.)

_____

_____

3. Older people are best suited to leadership roles due to their superior knowledge, experience and decision-making abilities.(改为强调句 It is… who)

_____

_____

4. The pressure releases the coffee oils.(改为强调句 It is… that)

_____

_____

5. The inspection process itself is likely to make the most difference.(改为强调句 It is… that)

_____

_____

6. When a journalist is willing to do whatever it takes to uncover the truth and inform the public, they can start to build a reputation as a reliable and believable reporter.(用 only when 改为倒装句)

_____

_____

7. Some people believe that universities and colleges should teach practical subjects that are deemed more related to employment.(It is believed by sb. that…)

_____

_____

8. People have long debated whether art courses should be made a compulsory part of the curriculum at high school. (It is debated whether ...)

_____

_____

9. Some claim that the construction process is faster, that waste is reduced and that there is less disruption to the environment.(It is claimed that ...)

_____

_____

10. Some people suggest that all the young adults should undertake a period of unpaid work helping people in the community. (It is suggested that...)

_____

_____

11. Because they lack driving experience, young drivers are more likely to adopt unsafe driving practices and fail to observe road hazards. (due to; one's lack of)

_____

_____

12. If there is not an honest disposition and strong moral principles to guide them, aspiring journalists will be destined for failure before they even begin their careers.(without)

_____

_____

13. As far as I am concerned, the government funding should not be confined to the scholarship for the best students.(be restricted to)

_____

_____

14. Being innovative and creative is good for problem-solving and prepares students for their future study. (be beneficial to)

_____

_____

15. Despite the many benefits of volunteer work, there are some drawbacks that have a tendency to stop young people from getting involved.(deter sb. from doing sth.)

_____

_____

16. The introduction of childcare centres has been controversial among working parents in recent years. (spark controversy)

_____

_____

17. Before the availability of television sets, people would spend greater amounts of leisure time outdoors in the local community.(prior to)

_____

_____

18. As long as there are taxpayers to offset the high costs associated with free public healthcare, there is no reason why we cannot all get medical treatment if and when needed. (have access to)

_____

_____

19. Governments must control the water supply and enforce restrictions when and where necessary. (It is imperative that...)

_____

_____

20. Although there are efforts of worldwide cooperation, individuals remain the necessary driving force behind long-term, sustainable solutions.(despite)

_____

_____

21. If democracy can work, then environmental action can work as well.(改为倒装句)

_____

_____

22. The number of single-person households has increased significantly.(There be句型+an increase in)

_____

_____

23. The social dynamics of local communities have shifted profoundly in recent years.(There be句型+a shift in)

_____

_____

24. The masses still regard art as an important form of creative expression.(改为被动句)

_____

_____

25. Since speeding and drink-driving offenders are not limited to the young driver age bracket, targeting these offences instead of targeting young drivers in general would have a greater impact on improving the overall level of road safety.(as opposed to)

_____

_____

26. No matter where we live in the world, we all tend to exist within a cultural bubble that reflects our surrounding environment and the people we interact with on a daily basis.(regardless of)

_____

_____

27. In my opinion, humanity should try their best to preserve the world's remaining languages at all costs.(endeavour to do sth.)

_____

_____

28. People often think of museums and historical sites as tourism attractions rather than places of interest that appeal to tourists and locals alike.(改为被动句)

_____

_____

29. We see vacation as a time to relax, enjoy ourselves and do things that we would not normally do at home.(改为被动句)

_____

_____

30. People who sit at home can research complicated issues with a few clicks of a mouse. (画线部分改为分词短语)

_____

_____

31. The crowd, which had been thin for the first half of the race, had now grown considerably.(画线部分改为分词短语)

_____

_____

32. Infrastructure is a major issue that continues to affect millions of people. (画线部分改为分词短语)

_____

_____

33. Growers, who noticed this trend, began growing more and more tulips with increasingly exotic sounding names and colours. (画线部分改为分词短语)

_____

_____

34. That means the stories that are submitted by users are not edited, fact-checked or screened before they post.(画线部分改为分词短语)

_____

_____

35. Knitting offered people from poor communities a way of making extra money <u>while they were doing other tasks</u>. (画线部分改为分词短语)

___

36. Among the changes has been the first aid equipment because of advances in technology.(owing to)

___

37. The reason for the crash was given as engine failure.(the cause of)

___

38. Damage may cause stunted (发育不足的) growth and sometimes death of the plant.(result in)

___

39. A poor diet will ultimately result in illness.(lead to)

___

40. As a result, services have been drastically (急剧) reduced.(for this reason)

___

41. Therefore, they were more likely to be influenced by the guesses that other people made.(consequently)

___

42. The other banks are going to be very eager to help, provided that they see that he has a specific plan. (on condition that)

___

43. So long as there was enough land and the economy kept growing, there were few problems. (as long as)

___

44. The theatre faces closure if it doesn't get an urgent cash injection.(unless)

___

45. People give various reasons and excuses for not regularly recycling.(on a regular basis)

46. The teacher should encourage the child to proceed as far as possible.(as… as sb. can)

47. The majority of people highly value their time and therefore resent the inconvenience of long commutes between frequented destinations, such as home, work, and school. (place a high value on sth.)

48. If you should be fired, your health and pension benefits would not be automatically cut off. (改为倒装句)

49. If it were that simple, mothers would be defined by those things alone.(改为倒装句)

50. If we had left the situation alone and done nothing, we would have been on the other side of it by now. (改为倒装句)

（答案见 pp. 129~141）

Test ①

改正例文中拼写错误的单词。

> **》 作文题目 《**
>
> Genetic engineering for both medical and agricultural purposes is causing an increasing amount of controversy. Discuss the advantages and disadvantages of genetic engineering and explain your opinion.
>
> 用于医疗和农业目的的转基因技术正在引起越来越多的争议。讨论转基因技术的利弊，并解释你的观点。

》 例文

① New advances in scientific technology have allowed sientists to develop the means to change the biological make-up of living organizms to engineer agriculturul and medicanal products. ② Clearly, there are both advantages and disadvantages of ginetic engineering, and I personally believe that genetic modification should be used to adapt medicanal products, but not agriculturul products.

③ There are many ethacal and health issues associated with genetic engineering, and it is a complex and highly controvertial issue. ④ I believe that genetic engineering is beneficial when used to develop new medacines or scientific technology that helps prolong people's lives. ⑤ For example, if a person is dyeing of an incurable diseese and genetic engineering technology can provide a new medacine or a treetment that will keep that person alive and well for several more years, then I beleive it should be used. ⑥ However, I think that teckniques like cloning are unethacal and potentially dangerous because the effects of these teckniques are unknown and largely unnecesary.

⑦ Genetic engineering has also been used to modify the biological features of agricultural produce. ⑧ For example, people preffer to buy bananas that are bright yellow because they look fresh and healthy. ⑨ Naturaly grown, organnic bananas, however, are not perfectly yellow, but often have naturally ocurring brown spots caused by sugar. ⑩ Scientists have developed methods of changing the jeans of bananas to prevent them from turning brown. ⑪ This sort of genetic engineering is unnecessary in my opinion, and may subject people to unnecessary risks since it has not yet been determuned what kinds of health risks the genetic changes might cause.

⑫ In conclushion, genetic modifickation should be used for necessary and useful purposes like saving lives, not for rearranging geanes to change the appearance of agricultural products, a potenshially dangerous and unnecessary procedure.

（答案见 p. 142）

Test ②

改正例文中的大小写错误，并补充标点符号，如逗号（ , ）、句号（ . ）和连字符（ - ）。

>> 作文题目 <<

Discuss the advantages and disadvantages of traditional food and fast food. Which type of food do you prefer and why?

讨论传统食品和快餐的优点和缺点。你喜欢哪种类型的食物，为什么？

>> 例文

① in our modern fast paced society traditional food has often been replaced by fast food alternatives ② there are advantages and disadvantages of both traditional and fast food meals but i prefer traditional food because it is healthier less expensive and more enjoyable to prepare eat and share

③ fast food has many advantages ④ firstly fast food restaurants like mcdonald's and burger king are plentiful and provide take away meals that can be consumed on the run so busy individuals do not have to sacrifice valuable time to eat their meals ⑤ pre packaged meals can also be prepared at home in minutes with little effort ⑥ however fast food also has its disadvantages ⑦ for example fast food is often expensive ⑧ fast food is frequently high in fat and salt which when consumed on a regular basis can contribute to health problems like obesity and high blood pressure

⑨ similarly traditional food also has advantages and disadvantages ⑩ the advantages of traditional food preparation are that the ingredients of a traditional meal are often healthy inexpensive in season and produced locally sustaining local farmers and growers ⑪ the seasonings added to traditional meals are usually varied and enrich the diet ⑫ one of the disadvantages of traditional cooking is that it often takes time and careful effort ⑬ some people may view this as an advantage however because cooking skills are developed during this process and the ingredients are well savoured while related traditions such as dining etiquette and family gathering are promoted

⑭ in my opinion while fast food is convenient and easy it is often unhealthy and expensive. ⑮ personally I prefer to spend a few extra minutes preparing a meal which is worth savouring and sharing than to indulge in expensive fast food meals that are greasy salty and in my opinion unsatisfying

（答案见 pp. 142~143）

在例文横线上填入适当的限定词，包括冠词（the）、不定冠词（a/an）、零冠词（/）、物主代词和数量词。

━━━━━━━━━━━━━ ❯❯ 作文题目 ❮❮ ━━━━━━━━━━━━━

Some people think that keeping animals in zoos is cruel to the animals, while others believe that zoos keep many animal species alive that would otherwise be extinct.

Explain both sides of this argument and give your opinion.

一些人认为把动物关在动物园里对动物很残忍，而另一些人则认为动物园让许多本来会灭绝的动物物种存活下来。

解释这一争论的正反面，并给出你的观点。

❯❯ 例文

① There are thousands of zoos around _____ world which house millions of animals worldwide.
② Many people think that keeping animals in _____ cage is cruel and unnatural, but others argue that zoos protect animals and that without zoos, many of _____ animals that are housed in them would be in danger of dying out. ③ I believe that _____ zoos are necessary to protect animals that would otherwise be endangered or extinct because of habitat loss.

④ In _____ past, it has often been considered cruel to confine wild animals to small cages purely for _____ amusement of curious human beings. ⑤ Many people believe that wild animals should be allowed to roam free in _____ natural habitats and to hunt their natural prey. ⑥ I also believe this would be ideal, but unfortunately, due to _____ humankind's prolific population on Earth, many animals' natural habitats have been destroyed and many wild animals' prey is no longer sufficient in number to sustain them. ⑦ Cities, towns and _____ industry have taken over land which was once home to _____ variety of different species.

⑧ Therefore, I agree with _____ sentiment that zoos have become necessary to protect and sustain many species which would have little or no chance of survival in _____ wild. ⑨ For example, _____ panda bear of China is _____ endangered species which has been successfully bred in zoos, thus helping to keep the species alive. ⑩ Similarly, tigers have grown in numbers since living in zoos, and _____ animals today have been bred in captivity. ⑪ Ideally, _____ manmade habitats of _____ zoo animals should replicate their natural habitats as much as possible. ⑫ Often, panda bear pens in zoos have bamboo available, so panda bears can feed on _____ favourite food as they would in _____ wild.

⑬ In conclusion, because many wild animals' natural habitats have been destroyed by humans, we can do our best to make _____ manmade environments in zoos as spacious and natural as possible to enable many endangered species to survive.

（答案见 pp. 143~144）

Test ❹

改正例文中的动词错误。

The quality of computer language translation has improved significantly in recent years. Therefore it is not necessary for children to learn a foreign language.

To what extent to you agree or disagree?

近年来，计算机语言翻译的质量有了很大的提高。因此，孩子们没有必要学习外语。
对此你在多大程度上同意或不同意？

>> 例文

① In recent years, computer technology had advanced significantly. ② Now we can communicate with people who spoke different languages with the use of computer translation software. ③ Despite the development of these useful resources, I disagree that children should not learn foreign languages because learning another language can help an individual not only better understanding their own language, but also communicating on both personal and cultural levels.

④ Firstly, learning a foreign language is often a helpful way to getting a better insight into one's own language. ⑤ For example, from personal experience, I found that learning Italian were useful in the acquisition of more vocabulary in my native language: Spanish. ⑥ While computers can help translate Spanish into Italian, if I exclusively used computers to translate for me, I would not have gained further knowledge of my own and other languages, like English and German, which also shares some similar word formations. ⑦ In this way, learning foreign languages had a lot of advantages beyond just communication.

⑧ Secondly, computerised translation software can help people translate foreign text or even conversing with a person who speaks a different language, but computers cannot communicate on a personal or cultural level. ⑨ For example, one of my closest friends speak Italian as a first language. ⑩ We could consult our computers to have a conversation, but our conversations are richer and more interesting when we attempt to communicating by actually speaking to each other. ⑪ Also, we are able to share the different aspects of our cultures and home countries, the taste of our native dishes and the expressions unique to our local dialects, which our computers cannot did.

⑫ In conclusion, I disagree with people who believed that computer translation is sufficient for communication between people who speak different languages. ⑬ I believe children should teach foreign languages to broaden their knowledge and to help them communicating with people of other cultures.

（答案见 p. 144）

用括号内名词的正确形式填空。

>> 作文题目 <<

The increase in the use of mobile phones in recent years has transformed the way we communicate, live, and do business. Mobile phones can also, however, be the cause of social or medical problems. What are some of the problems caused by mobile phone usage? Do you think the advantages of mobile phones outweigh the disadvantages?

近年来，手机使用频率的增加改变了我们沟通、生活和做生意的方式。然而，手机也可能导致社会或医疗问题。使用手机会带来哪些问题？你认为手机的好处大于坏处吗？

▶ 例文

① Over the past decade, the _____ (popularity) of mobile phones has increased exponentially, changing many _____ (aspect) of the way people live. ② Most people agree that the majority of these changes are positive, but there are also negative aspects of the _____ (overuse) of mobile phones. ③ In my opinion, the _____ (advantage) of mobile phones outweigh the _____ (disadvantage).

④ Mobile phones have become very widely used and have impacted the average person's _____ (lifestyle) in many positive ways. ⑤ Mobile phones make it easy for parents to keep in touch with their _____ (child). ⑥ Also, many people today have mobile phones which access the _____ (Internet), so they can not only make phone calls, but also send emails and conduct _____ (business) via their phones. ⑦ This is extremely advantageous as it means that people do not have to be confined to their homes or offices in order to get in touch with friends, family, or business associates; _____ (communication) can take place anywhere and at any time.

⑧ The prolific use of mobile phones can also have negative _____ (impact) on individuals and society, however. ⑨ For example, if children are given mobile phones to use when they are unsupervised, they may access inappropriate _____ (content) on the Internet. ⑩ In addition, some people who rely too heavily on Internet-equipped mobile phones might become more isolated than an individual who must rely on social interaction for their _____ (entertainment). ⑪ Some _____ (study) have also shown that the overuse of mobile phones can pose health risks like cancer, although additional _____ (research) needs to be conducted to prove this theory. ⑫ If people are aware of these _____ (downside) to mobile phone use, I believe they can take steps to prevent most social and medical problems from occurring.

⑬ In _____ (conclusion), in my opinion, mobile phones' advantages far outweigh their disadvantages.

（答案见 pp. 144~145）

在例文横线上填入适当的介词。

》 作文题目 《

The graph illustrates the varying number of tourists visiting New Zealand over a twelve-month period. Summarise the information by selecting and reporting the main features of the graph and make appropriate comparisons where relevant.

该图显示了12个月内访问新西兰的游客数量的变化。请通过选取、汇报该图的主要特征来总结图表信息，并在相关的地方进行适当的比较。

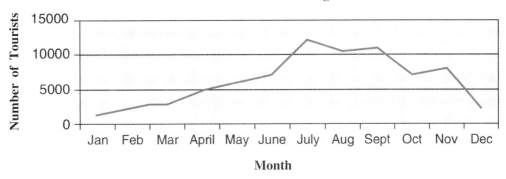

Number of Tourists Visiting New Zealand

Month

》 例文

① The line graph shows the amount _____ foreign tourists visiting New Zealand, measured _____ thousands of people. ② The graph is divided _____ twelve months. ③ Overall, the number of tourists was highest _____ July and lowest _____ December and January.

④ _____ January, the number of tourists was around one thousand for the month, and then increased slightly throughout February, reaching around three thousand _____ March. ⑤ _____ April, the number of tourists visiting New Zealand had risen _____ five thousand and continued to increase gradually _____ May and June, when it reached approximately seven thousand. ⑥ From there, the number of tourists increased dramatically, reaching a peak in July around twelve thousand tourists, the highest number of all the months shown. ⑦After July, the number of tourists decreased _____ just over ten thousand in August. ⑧ _____ September, the number of tourists had increased again slightly _____ around eleven thousand, but then began to decrease again _____ September. ⑨Tourist numbers declined markedly in October _____ around seven thousand and then increased _____ eight thousand in November. ⑩ Between November and December, the number of tourists visiting New Zealand decreased significantly _____ around two thousand _____ the end of the year.

（答案见 p. 145）

选择合适的词语，用其正确形式填空。

———— » **作文题目** «————

The two bar charts below illustrate the average yearly rainfall and average temperatures in four cities. Summarise the information by selecting and reporting the main features of the graph and make appropriate comparisons where relevant.

下面的两张柱状图显示了四个城市的年平均降雨量和平均气温。请通过选取、汇报该图的主要特征来总结图表信息，并在相关的地方进行适当的比较。

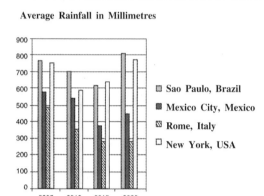

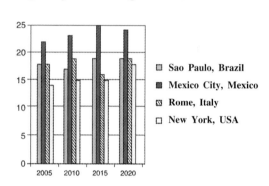

◎ **例文**

decrease	fluctuate	gradually	hover	increase	occur
range	reach	show	slightly	top	

① The two bar charts _____ the average rainfall in millimetres and the average temperatures in degrees Celsius in four cities in four separate years.

② In the first bar chart, Sao Paulo began with the highest average rainfall, with about 760 millimetres in 2005, an amount which _____ to around 600 millimetres in 2015 and then _____ again to around 805 millimetres in 2020, the highest amount shown on the chart. ③Mexico City showed a similar trend. ④In Rome, Italy, the highest rainfall fell in 2005 (just under 500 millimetres) and then the figures _____ decreased in each of the successive years, _____ just under 300 millimetres in 2020. ⑤New York had the next highest annual rainfall all the time except in 2015 when it _____ the list. ⑥In the other three years, its figures _____ from around 600 to 775 millimetres.

⑦ The second bar chart shows the average temperatures in degrees Celsius in the same four cities. ⑧ Mexico City recorded the highest annual temperature for each of the four years shown, with the highest temperature of 25 degrees Celsius _____ in 2015. ⑨ Temperatures in Sao Paulo and Rome _____ between 15 and 20 degrees Celsius for all four years. ⑩ New York, however, showed the lowest annual temperatures, which _____ around 15 degrees from 2005 to 2015 and rose _____ to about 17 degrees in 2020.

（答案见 p. 145）

阅读以下 5 分作文，改正文章中的错误。

>> 作文题目 <<

The bar chart illustrates the use of cash payment and electronic payments in New Zealand between 2013 and 2023. Summarise the information by selecting and reporting the main features of the graph and make appropriate comparisons where relevant.

该柱状图显示了 2013 年至 2023 年新西兰的现金支付和电子支付情况。请通过选取、汇报该图的主要特征来总结图表信息，并在相关的地方进行适当的比较。

Cash Payment vs. Electronic Payments

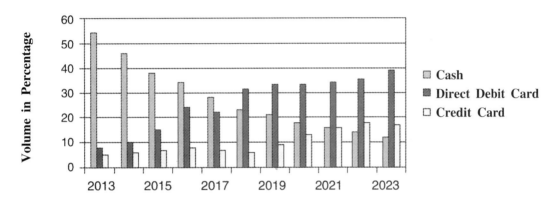

>> 例文

① This diagram show different transaction by cash, direct debit crd and credit card in each year from 2013 to 2023. ② There is a big difference between them.

③ Credit card was general low in all kinds of transaction but rise in 2022 and 2023 over cash. ④ Cash was highest at the beginning in 2013 and get smaller over time in graph. ⑤ By 2023, cash became the smallest. ⑥ It is around 10 percent of transaction. ⑦ direct debit card was low in 2013 but not low as credit card. ⑧ It was getting higher overall and 2018 to 2023 has surpassed credit card and cash. ⑨ On the whole, credit card remains relative stable, direct debit card go up and cash fall down.

（答案见 pp. 145~146）

阅读以下 6 分作文，改正文章中的语法错误并优化表达。

>> 作文题目 <<

Tourism is becoming so widespread that the number of tourists visiting old sites causes problems such as overcrowding, leading to the site being damaged and the quality of the experience of the visit being reduced.

To what extent do you agree that this is a problem and what can governments do to solve the problem?

旅游正变得如此流行，以至于参观旧址的游客数量造成了过度拥挤等问题，令景点遭到破坏，游览体验的质量降低。

你在多大程度上同意这是一个问题？政府可以做些什么来解决这个问题？

>> 例文

① Tourism has become the main type of entertainment, so the number of tourist has increased rapidly in recent years. ② However, some people say that excessive number of tourist visiting old sites will damage the site and the quality of tour will reduce. ③ I strongly agree with this viewpoint.

④ Firstly, people are easy to discover everything by themselves due to curiosity. ⑤ In old sites such as museums, there are lots of old and fragile things i.e. antiques or heritages. ⑥ With large crowds of tourists, it is difficult for the tour-guide to tell the visitors what they should do and what they should not do. ⑦ From that, the heritages and conserved things are easy haphazardly damaged by the visitors. ⑧ Secondly, too many visitors also affect the quality of the tour. ⑨ The tourists are from everywhere in the world, so different language is a big problem. ⑩ There is not enough well-informed tour-guide to instruct the tourists. ⑪ Additionally, to satisfy all the demands of the visitor is another disadvantage. ⑫ For example, in one tour, one visitor wants to visit in long period of time, but another feels hungry so he or she needs to enjoy their meals. ⑬ That causes difficulty for the tour-guide to organise and manage the tour.

⑭ One solution to decrease the negative effects of large crowds is to limit the number of visitors in one tour. ⑮ Another way is granting the policy to protect and conserve the heritages in old sites. ⑯ For example, do not allow the children visit such these places or do not let the tourists touch the things in old sites. ⑰ With these ways, I believe the damages in old sites will decrease.

⑱ In summary, it can be seen that overcrowding of visitors can easily make old sites being damaged and the quality of the visit reduced. ⑲ We should all try to make sure that this does not happen often in our tourism development.

（答案见 pp. 146~147）

阅读以下 5 分作文，改正文章中的语法错误并优化表达。

```
》》 作文题目 《《
```

Computers are widely used in education, and teachers now play a less important role in the classroom than ever before. Do you agree or disagree?

计算机在教育中被广泛使用，现在教师在课堂上发挥的作用比以往都要小。对此你是同意还是不同意？

》 例文

① In modern world, most students use the computers for the education widely, and people believe that teachers play less important role in classroom. ② I disagree with this. ③ I would like to talk about computer in education.

④ These days poeple are very busy because they are always go to school early in the morning and study in the classroom all day. ⑤ After school they usually go to private acadamy until midnight. ⑥ Under these circumstances they do not have spare time so that they cannot enjoy their activities. ⑦ All they do is study. ⑧ For taht reason using the computer education is very useful for students. ⑨ Computer education system makes much more free students because they can access when they want to need some information. ⑩ Moreover, computer educations are more extensive than school systems. ⑪ For these reasons, most student prefer to use the computer to learn.

⑫ In the opposite direction, some people worry aout computer education as students often play computers too much, such as computer games, email, entertainment and chat etc. ⑬ Some people say that nowadays student are exposure the computer communication too much, so they do not have to use computers even education. ⑭ Moreover, the teachers role has to more important than before. ⑮ Teachers could be control their students and encourage for their education.

（答案见 p. 147）

附录 雅思写作易拼错词

A

accommodation
according
account
achievement
achieving
across
advertisement
affect
afraid
aggressive
almost
although
ambulance
amount
apartment
apparently
appearance
approach
argument
aspect
attendant
attract
audience
Australia
available
awareness

B

beautiful
because
before
beginning
believe
beneficial
benefit
brought

Buddha
bullying
busy
business

C

calendar
capable
career
category
cemetery
century
choice
colleagues
committed
committee
communicate
compared
comparison
competition
completely
concentration
connected
conscious
constructive
continuously
control
convenient
correct
courses
culture
customs

D

definitely
degree
department

describe
development
difference
different
difficult
dilemma
disappear
disappoint
discuss
diseases
dormitory
doubled
dramatically
due

E

efficient
eliminate
embarrass
endless
energetic
energy
engineer
enormous
enough
environment
equal
especially
existence
experience

F

facilities
faithfully
family
familiar
finally

follow
foreigner
foreseeable
forward
fourth
furthermore
future

G

generally
glamorous
government

H

happiness
harmony
healthy
holiday
honorary
humorous
hygiene

I

illustrate
imagine
immediately
immigrant
inadvisable
incidentally
increased
independent
individual
industry
instead
intelligence
interested
interpret

K

kindergarten
kindness
knowledge

L

level
libraries
literacy
luxury

M

machine
manner
media
medium
million
museum

N

necessary
nineties
noise
noisy
non-existent
noticeable
nowadays
number

O

occasion
occasionally
occur
occurred
officer

often
opportunity
origin
otherwise

P

party
passions
pavilion
pension
people
percentage
period
persistent
Philippines
piece
pizza
politician
pollution
population
possession
possible
preferences
preferred
pressure
prevent
properly
property
proportion
punctuated

R

reached
receive
recommend

referred
relevant
religion
religious
remember
resistance
resources
responsibility
restaurant
reveal
revolution
rhythm
ridiculous

S

salary
scene
scholarship
second
sense
separate
similar
sincere
sincerely
somebody
something
special
spite
stability
standard
sterling
strength
struggling
succeed
success

suppressed
surprise
system

T

tattoo
technician
technology
tendency
temperature
theoretical
therefore
thieves
throughout
tomorrow
tongue
tourist
treatment
truly
twelfth
twentieth

U

unfortunately
university
until

V

view

W

weird
which

练习参考答案

第1章 7大常见语法错误

第1节 单词拼写错误

Exercise 1

1. disappear
2. throughout
3. beneficial
4. knowledge
5. technology
6. ambulance
7. travel
8. official
9. recommend
10. nutrition
11. kindergarten
12. pollution
13. university
14. weather
15. origin

Exercise 2

1. Children can easily be influenced by advertisements.

【译文】儿童容易受广告影响。

2. Tourism can damage local culture and be bad for the environment.

【译文】旅游业会破坏当地文化,对环境有害。

3. Social networking is common nowadays.

【译文】现在网络社交很普遍。

4. Many restaurants have to provide lower-cost meals in order to compete.

【译文】为了进行竞争,许多餐馆不得不供应低成本的餐食。

5. The Internet allows anybody to publish their own writing.

【译文】互联网允许任何人发表自己的文章。

6. The increase in the use of mobile phones has changed the way we do business.

【译文】手机使用频率的增加改变了我们做生意的方式。

7. They can take steps to prevent most social and medical problems from occurring.

【译文】他们可以采取措施以防止大部分社会和医疗问题的发生。

8. This acid rain can damage plants and animals in the countryside.

【译文】这场酸雨会破坏农村地区的动植物。

9. Job satisfaction is indeed very important for the well-being of a person.

【译文】工作满意度对一个人的幸福感确实非常重要。

10. Is it wise to allow employees to wear casual clothes?

【译文】允许员工穿便装明智吗?

11. The numbers for video rentals in the United States were the highest of all figures throughout the six-year period.

【译文】在整个六年间,美国的录像带租赁数是所有数值中最高的。

12. Motorways often go through beautiful areas and may damage plants and wildlife.

【译文】高速公路经常穿过风景优美的地区,可能会破坏植物和野生动物。

13. As a result, the earth's temperature is beginning to rise.

【译文】因此,地球的温度开始上升。

14. I believe the family is one of the most important structures in society.

【译文】我认为家庭是社会中最重要的结构之一。

15. Governments should provide money to artists of traditional music and art to maintain the strong tradition of the countries.

【译文】政府应该向传统音乐大师和传统艺术大师提供资金,以维护国家的深厚传统。

Exercise 3

1. The panda of China is an endangered species which has been successfully bred in zoos.

【译文】中国的大熊猫是濒危物种,它们在动物园里成功得到培育。

2. These customs are common in Muslim countries such as Saudi Arabia.

【译文】这些习俗在沙特阿拉伯等伊斯兰国家很常见。

3. **She** started to work for **Apple** in **May** 2023.
   【译文】她于2023年5月开始在苹果公司工作。

4. **I** went to university in **Geneva** in **Switzerland**.
   【译文】我在瑞士日内瓦上大学。

5. **They** took a taxi from **York Railway Station** to the **Royal York Hotel** in the city centre.
   【译文】他们从约克火车站乘出租车到市中心的皇家约克酒店。

6. **However**, **I** do not believe that we generally work longer hours than previously.
   【译文】不过，我认为我们的工作时间一般没有以前长。

7. **It** is hard to disagree with the suggestion that going to a better school gives a child a better chance at getting admitted to a better **university**.
   【译文】很难不同意这一说法，即上更好的学校会让孩子有更大的机会被更好的大学录取。

8. Americans do not take a long time for meals; they eat and drink for 1.5 **hours** each day.
   【译文】美国人花在吃饭上的时间不长；他们每天饮食时长为1.5小时。

9. **During** **spring**, people all over **Europe** are in gardens and **parks** watching wildlife and taking notes.
   【译文】在春天，欧洲各地的人们都在花园和公园里观赏野生动植物并做笔记。

10. **In** **January**, the number of tourists was around **one thousand** for the **month**, and then increased slightly throughout **February**.
    【译文】1月份，当月游客人数约为1,000人，然后在整个2月份略有增加。

第2节 标点使用错误

Exercise 1

1. Overall, I believe the advantages are stronger than the disadvantages.
   【译文】总的来说，我认为优势大于劣势。

2. After some time, it will fly away to begin its adult life and start the cycle again.
   【译文】一段时间后，它将飞走，开始它的成年生活，并再次开始这个循环。

3. C
   【译文】医生们认为传统药物比现代药物更健康、更有效。

4. Because of industrialisation and global trade, many traditions have disappeared.
   【译文】由于工业化和全球贸易，许多传统已经消失。

5. However, there are certainly dangers in taking time off at that important age.
   【译文】然而，在那个重要的年纪中断学业肯定是有风险的。

6. However careful you are, accidents can always happen.
   【译文】不管你多么小心，意外总是有可能发生的。

7. The graph illustrates changes in the amounts of beef, lamb, chicken, and fish consumed between 1999 and 2023.
   【译文】图表显示了1999年至2023年间牛肉、羊肉、鸡肉和鱼类消费量的变化。

8. C
   【译文】有些人因为怜悯那些必须生活在小笼子里的动物而拒绝去动物园。

9. Firstly, a person needs to feel that they are doing valued and valuable work, so positive feedback from superiors is very important in this respect.
   【译文】首先，一个人需要感觉到自己所做的工作得到重视并且有价值，所以上级的积极反馈在这方面非常重要。

10. More and more people, including young children, are seriously overweight.
    【译文】越来越多的人严重超重，包括年幼的儿童。

11. C
    【译文】我同意政府应该资助国民的文化追求。

12. In the UK, for example, there is currently a shortage of plumbers.

【译文】例如，在英国，目前水管工短缺。

13. C

【译文】信息技术和工程等部门需要技术人员。

14. Use of water per head of population has also increased as people all over the world use more water-consuming items, such as washing machines and flush toilets.

【译文】由于全世界范围内，人们使用的耗水物品比以前多，如洗衣机和抽水马桶，所以人均用水也有所增加。

15. Fast food is frequently high in fat and salt, which, when consumed on a regular basis, can contribute to health problems like obesity and high blood pressure.

【译文】快餐经常是高脂高盐食物，如果经常食用，会导致肥胖和高血压等健康问题。

Exercise 2

1. As a result of globalisation, the world's cultures are becoming less diverse; people are adopting the customs of countries with strong economies.

【译文】由于全球化，世界文化的多样性越来越低；人们正在采纳经济发达国家的风俗习惯。

2. Expected growth in luxury sales for other regions **is** Middle East (8.75%), North America (6%), Europe (3.75%), and Japan (1.75%).

【译文】其他地区的奢侈品销售额预期增长幅度为中东(8.75%)、北美(6%)、欧洲(3.75%)和日本(1.75%)。

3. Some people argue that happiness can be found in other aspects of life **such as** work, family, or hobbies.

【译文】有些人认为，幸福可以在生活的其他方面找到，比如工作、家庭或爱好。

4. There are many reasons for this; some people blame the amount of junk food that is available, and others **claim it is because** children don't get enough exercise.

【译文】造成这种情况的原因有很多。一些人指责能够买到的垃圾食品数量太多，另一些人则声称这是因为儿童没有得到足够的锻炼。

5. The song *Peace, Love and Happiness* is dedicated to the children he met there.

【译文】《和平、爱与幸福》这首歌是献给他在那里遇到的孩子们的。

6. There are two main types of training: behavioural and obedience.

【译文】训练主要有两类：行为训练和服从性训练。

7. It is **important** to make sure **that** other people know they cannot pet **him** or reward **him** if he jumps up.

【译文】重要的是要确保其他人知道，如果他跳起来，他们不能抚摸他或奖励他。

8. C

【译文】推行体育活动的费用其实可以相当低，比如，像我所在的地方议会所做的那样，在公园里安装锻炼设施。

9. Colour blindness, as a matter of fact, is more common among men than women.

【译文】事实上，色盲在男性中比在女性中更常见。

10. Leeds University, which was founded in 1904, has an excellent reputation.

【译文】利兹大学成立于1904年，声誉卓著。

第3节 名词错误

Exercise 1

1. U   2. C   3. C   4. U   5. U   6. C
7. C   8. U   9. C   10. C/U 11. C/U 12. U
13. C   14. U   15. C/U 16. U   17. C/U 18. U
19. C   20. U

Exercise 2

1. damages改为damage；are改为is

【译文】有些对于环境的破坏是永久性的。

【解析】damage作名词表示"破坏"时，为不可数名词，故此处应去掉-s。相应地，谓语动词需要遵循主谓一致的原则改用单数形式的is。

2. C

【译文】企业不应该从水资源中获利。

3. C

【译文】核武器有被恐怖分子获取的风险。

4. times改为time

【译文】城市的交通问题增加了上班和上学路程所花的时间。

【解析】此处time表示"时间"，为不可数名词，故应去掉-s。

5. pleasures改为pleasure

【译文】如果大学教育的重点是从学习中获得乐趣，那么学生们会更快乐。

【解析】pleasure表示"愉悦，快乐"时，为不可数名词，故此处应去掉-s。

6. knowledges改为knowledge

【译文】随着这些回收知识的传播，公众将会学习并对之有更好的了解。

【解析】knowledge为不可数名词，故此处应去掉-s。

7. phenomena改为phenomenon

【译文】人们应该警惕这种新现象，不要让它抑制面对面的互动。

【解析】phenomenon为可数名词，其复数形式为phenomena。此句中phenomena前有限定词this，故应用单数形式phenomenon。

8. works改为work

【译文】虽然独立学习有一定好处，但我认为小组合作通常更有成效。

【解析】group work意为"小组合作"，为不可数名词，故此处应去掉work后的-s。

9. informations改为information

【译文】该表提供了男性和女性在不同的主流跑步项目中的速度和距离信息。

【解析】information为不可数名词，故此处应去掉-s。

10. advices改为advice

【译文】救助协会的成员可以相互鼓励，分享个人故事，并在需要时提供建议。

【解析】advice为不可数名词，故此处应去掉-s。另外，此句中的time表示"时刻"，为可数名词，故用times无误。

Exercise 3

1. organisations

【译文】有人认为慈善机构应当救助那些最有需要的人，无论他们生活在哪里。

【解析】organisation为可数名词，而且在句子中泛指所有的慈善机构，但前面没有限定词a或the，故要用复数organisations表示泛指。

2. experiences

【译文】人是由其所见所闻所感这些经历所塑造的。

【解析】通过后面的what they see, hear and feel可知此处experience表示"经历，体验"，为可数名词。此处指很多经历，故用复数experiences。

3. research

【译文】动物被用于重要的科学研究。

【解析】research"研究"为不可数名词，故此处用其原形。

4. traffic

【译文】古建筑、寺庙和纪念碑难以应付巨大的客流量，并因此遭受到破坏。

【解析】traffic"人流"为不可数名词，故此处用其原形。

5. literature

【译文】女学生最喜欢的科目是技术性较弱的科目，如社会科学、语言、文学和人文学科。

【解析】literature"文学"为不可数名词，故此处用其原形。

6. frustration

【译文】由于交通堵塞会造成污染并且让人感到恼火，人们显然需要采取紧急行动。

【解析】frustration表示"沮丧"时，为不可数名词，故此处用其原形。

7. aid

【译文】我们可以更快地向受干旱、饥荒和疾病影响的地区提供援助，挽救许多人的生命。

【解析】aid"援助"为不可数名词，故此处用其原形。

8. furniture

【译文】最后，计划的建造工程还将包括安装一些厨房家具。

【解析】furniture"家具"为不可数名词,故此处用其原形。

9. education

【译文】因此,人们一致认为,技术是一种非常有价值的教育工具。

【解析】education"教育"为不可数名词,故此处用其原形。

10. employment

【译文】除了就业或继续深造,选择其他去向的学生相对少很多。

【解析】employment"就业"为不可数名词,故此处用其原形。

第4节 限定词错误

Exercise 1

1. **Many**

【译文】许多父亲和母亲共同养育子女,分担家务。

【解析】所修饰的名词fathers and mothers"父亲和母亲"为可数名词的复数,故选Many。

2. **their**

【译文】资助艺术家可以帮助他们充分发挥潜能,公众也能受益。

【解析】根据句意,此处缺少一个修饰potential的形容词性物主代词,因此选择their,指代"艺术家的"。

3. **the**

【译文】我们只研究了已知物种中的5%。

【解析】species后带有一个定语从句we know,可知是某一类确定的species,为特指,故选择定冠词the。

4. **much**

【译文】有人说这对教学和学习是有益的,因为有这么多的信息可用。

【解析】information是不可数名词,因此用much修饰。

5. **all your**

【译文】可以用它储存你所有的互联网密码。

【解析】all为前位限定词,your为中位限定词,因此修饰同一个名词passwords时,all在your前面。

Exercise 2

1. key改为the key

【译文】教育是事业成功的关键。

2. major issue 改为a major issue

【译文】贫穷是许多发展中国家的一个主要问题。

3. The pollution改为Pollution; the many cities改为many cities

【译文】在许多城市,污染是一个严重的问题。

4. A people改为People

【译文】人们应该能够自由地表达自己的意见。

5. the children改为children; in the life改为in life

【译文】教育对孩子们在一生中取得成功很重要。

6. a free healthcare改为free healthcare

【译文】政府应该为所有公民提供免费医疗。

7. the renewable energy sources改为renewable energy sources

【译文】政府需要对可再生能源进行投资。

8. country改为a country; its the history 改为its history

【译文】一个国家的文化是由它的历史和传统所塑造的。

9. The technology改为Technology; the others改为others

【译文】技术改变了我们与他人交流的方式。

10. The social media 改为Social media; the friends 改为friends

【译文】社交媒体已经成为一种与朋友联系的普遍方式。

第5节 动词错误

Exercise 1

1. **is**

【译文】有大量证据表明儿童有超重情况,而且情况越来越糟糕。

【解析】There be句型当中,be动词的单复数形式由其后真正的主语决定,且遵循"就近原则"。本句中主语为plenty of evidence,而evidence为不可数名词,故谓语动词用单数is。

2. has

【译文】我认为, 采取中间立场是明智的, 因为这每种方式都有其优势。

【解析】主语含有each of, 为单数, 故用has。

3. are

【译文】年轻人尤其愿意接受这个理念。

【解析】"the+形容词"表示一类人时, 谓语动词用复数形式。The young表示"年轻人"这个群体, 所以填are。

4. has

【译文】但最初在公共事务中毫不重要的事情现在已经发展成为一场社会运动。

【解析】what引导的从句作主语, 谓语动词用单数形式。

5. drive

【译文】好莱坞设想拥有邪恶思想的机器控制大批杀手机器人的理论很愚蠢。

【解析】空格要填的谓语动词属于同位语从句, 该从句的主语是machines with evil minds, 介词短语with evil minds为machines的定语, 因此主语的中心词为machines, 是复数, 所以用drive。

6. is

【译文】参加各项活动的本科毕业生人数多于研究生人数。

【解析】The number of...作主语, 谓语动词用单数形式。

7. are

【译文】而且, 父亲和母亲都开始意识到双方有选择育儿角色的自由。

【解析】both... and连接两个名词作主语, 是复数, 所以用are。

8. has/have

【译文】公众才有力量使这种破坏性的政策无利可图并失去合法性。

【解析】本句为强调句, 主语为集合名词the public, 在句子中的含义可理解为单数的"公众整体", 也可以理解为复数的"公众里的每个人", 所以谓语动词用单复数形式皆可。

9. go

【译文】很少有孩子去上学, 尤其是贫穷的孩子, 所以他们通过其他方式学习。

【解析】few修饰可数名词复数children作主语, 所以谓语动词用复数形式的go。

10. is; is

【译文】哪里能获得可靠的水源, 哪里就有很大的农业发展潜力。

【解析】access和potential都是不可数名词, 两者的谓语动词都用单数形式。

Exercise 2

1. was

【译文】2006年至2007年间, 到法国度假的人数略有增加。

【解析】通过时间状语between 2006 and 2007可以判断句子应使用一般过去时, 主语a slight increase为单数名词, 故填was。

2. will be

【译文】据预测, 从2020年到2040年, 滑雪度假的人数将急剧增加。

【解析】通过时间状语From 2020 to 2040以及主句的动词is predicted可以判断事件未发生, 仅为预测, 因此句子应该使用一般将来时, 故填will be。

3. have decreased

【译文】自2020年以来, 海滩度假的游客已从400多万逐渐减少到350万。

【解析】时间状语since 2020意思为"自从2020年起", 句子应该用现在完成时。主语Beach holidays为复数名词, 故此空填have decreased。

4. had gone down/went down

【译文】1990年后的30年里, 住宿费用逐渐下降。

【解析】时间状语for thirty years after 1990指过去1990年至2020年这段时间, 也可以简单理解为过去的时间, 所以句子时态用过去完成时或一般过去时皆可, 故填had gone down或went down。

5. shows; visited

【译文】图表显示了2009年夏天有多少游客游览了三个国家。

【解析】主句概述图表内容, 时态应该用一般现在时。主语graph为单数名词, 因此谓语用shows。宾语从句出现表示过去的时间状语in the summer of 2009, 因此谓语用过去式visited。

Exercise 3

1. B

【译文】政府计划全面禁烟。

【解析】plan后接动词不定式to do,表示"计划做某事"。

2. C

【译文】如果每个人选择每周至少步行两次,这可能会对污染水平产生重大影响。

【解析】decide后接动词不定式to do,表示"决定做某事"。

3. A

【译文】不幸的是,许多人因为生活繁忙而无法抗拒使用汽车。

【解析】resist后接动名词doing,表示"抗拒做某事"。

4. C

【译文】许多人喜欢开车,但他们应该尽量多走路。

【解析】enjoy后接动名词doing,表示"享受做某事"。try后接动词不定式to do,表示"努力做某事"。

5. D

【译文】我做完研究了,所以我需要开始写论文了。

【解析】finish后接动名词doing,表示"完成做某事"。start后接动名词doing或动词不定式to do皆可,都表示"开始做某事"。

Exercise 4

1. to perform

【译文】大多数年份我们都有一个儿童合唱团,但今年当地的军校学员主动提出要表演。

【解析】offer to do sth.表示"主动提出做某事"。

2. training

【译文】人们有时在开始时没有意识到的是,一周又一周地保持训练需要很大的决心和努力。

【解析】keep doing sth.表示"保持做某事"。

3. to have

【译文】如今,越来越多的人决定晚育。

【解析】decide to do sth.表示"决定做某事"。

4. to do/doing; to respect/respecting; to collect

【译文】所以,当我开始自己做一些家务时,我开始尊重别人的工作,并尽量在玩完玩具后收拾好所有的玩具。

【解析】begin to do/doing sth.表示"开始做某事"。try to do sth.表示"努力做某事"。

5. to rescue

【译文】尽管试图令全世界脱贫是一项令人钦佩的事业,但我坚持认为慈善机构应当把力气集中于服务当地民众上。

【解析】attempt to do sth.表示"试图做某事"。

第6节 介词错误

Exercise 1

1. of

【译文】许多有天赋的儿童被剥夺了挑战智力的机会。

【解析】固定搭配be deprived of意为"丧失"。

2. on

【译文】需要受教育水平高还是技能经验取决于你所申请的职位。

【解析】固定搭配depend on意为"取决于"。

3. for

【译文】说到底,只要人们愿意支持预防犯罪的举措,并为自身安全负责,总有办法减少犯罪的。

【解析】固定搭配take responsibility for意为"为……负责"。

4. to

【译文】相反,许多人默认我们对于预防犯罪是无能为力的。

【解析】固定搭配resign oneself to意为"顺从接受"。

5. with

【译文】在同一行业工作20年以上的人无疑已面对过很多艰难的抉择。

【解析】固定搭配be faced with意为"面对"。

Exercise 2

1. about改为of

【译文】然而,许多人对记者持谨慎态度,不愿相信他们的报道。

【解析】此处错误为介词搭配错误,be wary of意为"对……感到警惕",介词用of。

2. to改为on

【译文】在世界上的许多地区，温度和气候对公众健康产生不良影响。

【解析】此处错误为介词搭配错误，have effects on sth./sb.意为"对某事/某人有影响"，介词用on。

3. for改为of

【译文】家长是否应当主动参与到孩子读写能力的培养过程中，这个问题值得讨论。

【解析】此处错误为介词搭配错误，"……的问题"应该使用the question of。

4. at改为to

【译文】富有革新意识和创造性有助于培养解决问题的能力，为学生的深造做好准备。

【解析】此处错误为介词搭配错误，be beneficial to意为"有助于"，介词用to。

5. dedicate themselves in改为dedicate themselves to

【译文】在我看来，人不能指望依靠金钱或容貌成功，而是必须全身心地投入工作，增强适应力，从不言弃。

【解析】此处错误为介词搭配错误，dedicate oneself to意为"献身于"，介词用to。

6. from改为of

【译文】受到人类的直接影响，成千上万的动植物物种现在已经灭绝，而且灭绝的速度还在逐年增加。

【解析】此处错误为介词搭配错误，as a result of意为"是……的结果"，介词用of。

7. to learn改为to learning

【译文】为了为养育小孩这一终生任务做好充足准备，准父母应当保证学习成为称职父母的必备技能。

【解析】commit to (doing) sth.意为"保证做某事"，to是介词，因此后面的动词应用doing形式。

8. secure改为securing

【译文】大学的扩招除了能帮助更多年轻人培养日后生活和工作所需的技能，增加他们获得高薪工作的机会，也为未来的雇主扩充高技能候选人的储备。

【解析】secure在这个句子中是动词，意为"获得，得到"，因为跟在介词of后面，因此需要使用doing形式。

Exercise 3

1. The table shows a fall of 10% in primary school numbers.

【译文】该表显示小学人数下降了10%。

2. The government hopes to achieve a reduction in the number of cars coming into cities.

【译文】政府希望减少进城的汽车数量。

3. Since the introduction of digital communication technology, there has been a rise of 30% in electronic device usage.

【译文】自从引入数字通信技术以来，电子设备的使用量增长了30%。

4. The number of newly graduated students in Britain reached a peak of around 195,000 in 1997.

【译文】英国的应届毕业生人数在1997年到达顶峰，约195,000人。

5. Some people say that the best way to make an improvement in public health is by increasing the number of sports facilities.

【译文】有人说，增强公众健康的最好办法是增加体育设施的数量。

第7节 混淆连词和副词

Exercise 1

1. 删去and之后的逗号

【译文】瓶装水现在是一项价值1,000亿美元的业务，而且81%的瓶子没有被回收。

【解析】and是连词，用于连接两个并列分句时，其后无须加逗号。

2. 删去but后的逗号

【译文】人类的进化以及技术的进步使世界变得更美好，但这是破坏环境换来的。

【解析】but是连词，连接两个分句时后面不用加逗号。

3. 将however前的逗号改为句号，并且however的首字母大写；或把however改为but，并将其后的逗号删去

【译文】在过去，人们主要的学习方式是看书。然而，互联网改变了我们获取信息的途径，因此让书本变得过时了。

【解析】此处的 however 表转折，是副词，不可放在两个完整分句之间起连接的作用。因此，需要把两个分句变成独立的句子才能使用 however，或者使用连词 but 连接两个分句。

4. 在 therefore 前加 and；或将 therefore 前的逗号改为句号，therefore 首字母大写，therefore 后加逗号

【译文】通常的情况是，犯罪行为是由社会或环境因素造成的。因此，认为罪犯是天生的而不是后天塑造的这一论点并不成立。

【解析】therefore 是副词，要么放句中，与 and 连用，and 作为连词，连接两个分句；或者放句子开头，修饰句子，表示结果。

5. 删去 so 后的逗号

【译文】据估计，交通运输占能源消耗的 30%，因此降低对耗能车辆的需求对于减少出行对环境的影响至关重要。

【解析】so 是连词，连接分句时，其后无须加逗号。

6. 删去 Because 前的句号，Because 的首字母小写

【译文】有些人认为通过考试(的重要性)被过分强调，因为学生们在学校的大部分时间都花在了考试上，而不是学习上。

【解析】because 是连词，此处 Because 前后两个句子存在因果关系，可以直接使用 because 连接合为一个句子，because 前后无须加标点符号。

Exercise 2

1. however

【译文】然而，政府的财政支持也应用于保证大学的质量，因为学费和捐款不是固定的资金来源，也不一定足够。

2. Although

【译文】尽管学校财产遭受相当严重的破坏，但我认为，在这起事件中，判罚与罪行相符，避免将男孩收监是合理的。

3. In contrast

【译文】相反，当我们做自己喜欢的事情，热爱自己所做的事情时，我们会充满动力，迫不及待地开始每天的工作。

4. Moreover

【译文】社交媒体的兴起改变了我们与他人沟通和联系的方式。此外，它还深切影响了我们看待世界的方式。

5. Therefore

【译文】许多国家正在实施减少碳排放和应对气候变化的措施。因此，个人也必须改变日常习惯，以减少碳足迹。

第2章　如何写出正确的句子

第1节　如何扩充简单句

Exercise 1

1. major

【译文】大多数经理可以识别当前的大趋势。

2. one of

【译文】全球变暖是现代生活中最严重的问题之一，也影响着人们的健康和福祉。

3. for

【译文】越来越多的年轻人搬到城市，既为了寻找工作机会，也为了追求他们能在城市获取到的一切设施和机会。

4. made

【译文】个人造成的影响会是微乎其微的。

5. to enhance

【译文】儿童可以使用积分来增强电子游戏里的各种虚拟技能。

6. abrupt

【译文】我们观察到大约 4,100 年前发生了突变。

7. to purify; by

【译文】树木具有通过去除有害污染物和过滤有害气味来净化空气的非凡能力。

8. Starting; steep

【译文】从 1992 年的大约 165,000 人开始，英国的应届毕业生人数在接下来的五年里呈现出急剧上升的趋势。

Exercise 2

1. running

2. considerable; patients'; of doctors and drugs

3. private; to cover

4. living; with other communities

5. caused; effective

Exercise 3

1. 【扩1】New Zealand is a **small** country.

   【扩2】New Zealand is a small country **of four million inhabitants**.

2. 【扩1】Mobile communication offers a way for us **to pass time**.

   【扩2】Mobile communication offers a way for us to pass time **during various waiting periods**.

3. 【扩1】Coach launched the **lower-priced** Poppy handbags.

   【扩2】**Using these insights**, Coach launched the lower-priced Poppy handbags.

4. 【扩1】Governments should continue to support **professional** athletes.

   【扩2】Governments should continue to support professional athletes **with specialized training facilities**.

5. 【扩1】**Without enough green space**, a city is a concrete jungle.

   【扩2】Without enough green space, a city **covered with high-rise residential complexes** is a concrete jungle.

第2节 写出正确的并列句

Exercise 1

1. **so**

   【译文】博物馆很贵,所以很多人都去不起。

   【解析】并列连词前后语句之间是因果关系,前为因,后为果,故选so。

2. **and**

   【译文】由于地球上庞大的人口数量,许多动物的自然栖息地遭到破坏,许多野生动物的猎物数量已经不足以维持这些动物的生存。

【解析】并列连词前后语句是平等的内容,都是人口数量过多导致的后果,故选and。

3. **but**

   【译文】一些人认为把不同能力的孩子放在一起教育对他们都有好处,但另一些人认为聪明的孩子应该分开教,并给予特殊对待。

   【解析】并列连词前后语句是相反的内容,意思发生转折,故选but。

4. **yet**

   【译文】总而言之,正如我们所看到的,一些计划正在蓬勃开展,但许多计划却缺乏资金和其他基本资源。

   【解析】并列连词前后语句间是转折关系,选yet。

5. **as a result**

   【译文】如果年轻人不了解他们的文化遗产,他们就不会理解老一辈人,从而在文化群体内部可能会出现严重的沟通障碍。

   【解析】连接词前后语句之间是因果关系,前为因,后为果,故选as a result。

6. **for example**

   【译文】这些问题对保健和教育产生了负面影响。例如,我的母亲担心,如果食品价格继续上涨,她将无法为家人做健康的饭菜。

   【解析】连接词前的分句阐述观点,其后是在举例子,故选for example。

7. **otherwise**

   【译文】所以我们必须有一个全球计划;否则很可能会有灾难性的后果。

   【解析】连接副词后引出另一种可能性,用otherwise。

8. **therefore**

   【译文】这些品质不是男性或女性特有的,因此两性都能成功地抚养孩子。

   【解析】连接副词前后语句是因果关系,前为因,后为果,故选therefore。

9. **however**

   【译文】几年前,去当地公园会看到有人在踢足球或遛狗。然而,现在人们开始去健身房或玩攀岩墙,作为一种休闲运动方式。

   【解析】连接副词前后语句是转折关系,用however。

10. furthermore

【译文】首先,人们需要改变。此外,我们需要克服障碍,实现我们的目标。

【解析】连接副词前后语句是递进关系,因此要用furthermore。

Exercise 2

1. C

【译文】我们还没有赢;然而,我们将继续努力。

2. otherwise改为therefore或其他引出结果的连接词

【译文】首先,重要的是要记住,这是一个发展非常迅速的行业,所以很难做出明确的预测。

3. C

【译文】据估计,到2050年,农业产量需要翻一番,但气候变化是阻碍这一目标实现的主要威胁。

4. yet改为or或otherwise

【译文】当然,公司可能会损失一部分利润,但客户的安全必须放在第一位;否则,客户会转向另一家公司,再也不会回来。

5. because改为but或yet

【译文】没有人会否认名人工作努力、技术熟练,但他们并不比其他成千上万没有成名机会的工人更努力。

Exercise 3

1. First, swimming alone is against the rules; **moreover**, it is dangerous.

【译文】首先,独自游泳是违反规定的;此外,这很危险。

2. It cost the company a lot of money, **but** it saved the clients.

【译文】这让公司花了很多钱,但挽留了公司的客户。

3. Children have some advantages living in a big city; **for example**, they have more opportunities to choose what they want to do.

【译文】孩子们住在大城市里有一些好处。例如,他们有更多的机会选择他们想做的事情。

4. The solution is for government to encourage the use of public transport in urban areas; **thus**, people will be less dependent on their cars.

【译文】解决办法是政府鼓励在城市地区使用公共交通,从而减少人们对私人汽车的依赖。

5. Americans believed the next most important quality for men was ambition; **in contrast**, the next most important characteristic for women leaders was to be creative.

【译文】美国人认为对于男性而言,第二重要的品质是野心;相比之下,女性领导第二重要的品质是创造力。

第3节 写出正确的三大从句

Exercise 1

1. who/that; that/in which/不填; that/which

【译文】同样,收集玩偶的人可能不仅仅是扩大他们的收藏,而是对玩偶的制作方式或使用的材料也产生兴趣。

【解析】此句填的都是定语从句的关系词。第一个空格前面先行词是people(人),且在从句中作主语,因此使用who或that作为关系词。第二个空格前面先行词是way,在从句中作方式状语,固定使用的关系词为that、in which,也可省去不写。第三个空格前面先行词是materials(物),且在从句中作主语,因此使用that或which作为关系词。

2. Although/While; where

【译文】虽然由于疫苗的改进和医疗保健的普及,许多影响人类的疾病已经被根除,但世界上仍存在一些地区,在那里,一些健康问题更为普遍。

【解析】逗号前后的分句存在转折的逻辑关系,因此逗号前应该是让步状语从句,放在句首引导让步状语从句用Although或者While,表示"虽然"。第二个空格后的内容是修饰areas的定语从句,因为先行词areas在从句中作状语,表示地点,因此使用where作为关系词。

3. When; which

【译文】当我们设想讲故事这个动作时,我们通常会想到睡前故事,这些故事通常由父母读给孩子听,是一种哄孩子入睡的方法。

【解析】when引导时间状语从句,意为"当……时候"。which引导非限制性定语从句,修饰bedtime stories,关系词在从句中作主语。

4. that

【译文】即便如此，我仍然认为培养一群有自主阅读能力的年轻人是一个有价值的理想。

【解析】空格后是一个意思完整的分句，推测其为及物动词maintain的宾语从句，故填that引导。

5. who/that; that

【译文】有一些人确信，人类对野生动植物造成的危害是不可逆转的。

【解析】这道题可以先从第二个空格入手，第二个空格后的分句意思完整，推测是convinced的宾语从句，故填that引导。第一个空格前句子结构完整，空格后的内容是对those的补充说明，推测为定语从句。由convinced"确信的"可知those指人，且先行词在从句中作主语，故关系词用who或that。

6. because/as

【译文】有些人认为应该强制要求学习外语，因为它有助于智力发展。

【解析】两个分句之间是因果关系，空格后的分句表示原因，因此应使用because、as等词引导原因状语从句。

7. which

【译文】图表显示了2018年英国本科生和研究生在大学毕业后除了全职工作之外参加的活动信息。

【解析】空格前的介词in实际上是从句谓语动词participated in的一部分。该谓语动词的宾语是the activities，所以空格后的分句是the activities的定语从句，故关系词填which。

8. where

【译文】英国就是一个典型的例子，该国将烟民买烟的钱用于治疗肺癌和心脏病。

【解析】The United Kingdom在从句中充当地点状语，表示"在英国"，因此定语从句用where引导。

Exercise 2

1. 删去it

【译文】银行努力提高客户信心，因为他们的业务依赖于客户信心。

【解析】关系代词which已指代先行词customer confidence，因此定语从句中不需要再用it指代同样的内容，否则会造成成分赘余。

2. is改为are

【译文】许多国家没有资金建造海水淡化厂，因为海水淡化厂的建造成本很高。

【解析】定语从句也要遵循主谓一致原则，先行词是plants，为复数名词，因此从句中的谓语动词应用复数形式。

3. 删去when前面的逗号

【译文】当景点涌入过多人流时，自然资源往往会被过度开发。

【解析】when引导时间状语从句放在主句之后时，when前面不加逗号。

4. 删去although或but

【译文】如今，旅游业虽然为许多国家创造了很大一部分国民收入，但也存在一些弊端。

【解析】although和but不能同时使用，故只保留其一。

5. 删去because或so

【译文】总之，因为许多野生动物的自然栖息地遭到人类破坏，所以我们可以尽我们最大的努力在动物园里为它们提供尽可能宽敞和自然的人工环境。

【解析】because和so不能同时使用，故只保留其一。

Exercise 3

1. The bar chart gives information about the percentages of both men and women **who** consumed five types of fruits and vegetables each day in Britain.

【译文】该柱状图显示了英国每天食用五种果蔬的男女比例。

2. It can be seen that manufacture of olive oil is a complex process involving many steps and many devices.

【译文】可以看出，生产橄榄油是一个复杂的过程，需要很多步骤和设备。

3. This will mean that some people are unable to afford healthcare, **which** is why I disagree with the user-pays system.

【译文】这意味着有些人会承担不起医疗费用，这就是我为什么不同意个人自付的原因。

4. **When** people see or hear a well-known figure asking for their help, they are more likely to make a donation or volunteer their time to furthering the charity's work.

或：People are more likely to make a donation or volunteer their time to furthering the charity's work **when** they see or hear a well-known figure asking for their help.

【译文】若看到或听到名人呼吁大家给予援助，人们更有可能进行捐赠或者自愿花时间推广慈善工作。

5. **It is foreseeable that** we will come to rely on machines to complete dangerous or repetitive tasks to an even greater extent soon.

【译文】可以预见，我们不久就会在更大程度上依赖机器去完成危险的或重复的工作。

Exercise 4

1. **It can be observed that** the loss of energy produced by brown coal is slightly higher than that by black coal.

2. In the 21st century, more and more people are opting to live alone **if** they can afford to do so.

3. The table compares the percentage of people **who** lived in different types of residences in Australia in two years: 2012 and 2017.

4. **Although** recycling is an expensive and time-consuming process, it is one solution for protecting the environment from further destruction.

5. **There is no evidence to suggest that** banning certain food advertising would lead to a significant reduction in the rate of overeating for the world's population.

第4节 写出正确的被动句

Exercise 1

write—written   invite—invited
cause—caused   damage—damaged

take—taken   invent—invented
cut—cut   grow—grown
attend—attended   set—set
bring—brought   construct—constructed
think—thought   catch—caught
blow—blown   steal—stolen
break—broken   freeze—frozen
choose—chosen   forget—forgotten
wake—woken   know—known
rise—risen   mistake—mistaken

Exercise 2

1. is given

【译文】有人提供有关出售照片的建议。

2. have been written

【译文】那位教授为学生写了很多关于学习技巧的书。

3. had been converted

【译文】这条小路已改建为一条大路，并向东延伸。

4. were taken

【译文】在20世纪之前，总共估计有200,000只动物从群岛上被带走。

5. are being tested

【译文】各行各业——无论是艺术家、海洋生物学家还是天文学家——每天都在试探未知的边界。

Exercise 3

1. It claims改为It is claimed；should not use改为should not be used

【译文】有人认为，政府对大学的资助只应用于给最优秀的学生颁发奖学金，不作他用。

2. have identify改为have been identified

【译文】从那时起，大约有25个热门地区被确定为保护的主要目标。

3. should spend改为should be spent

【译文】其他人认为，这笔钱应该用于改善现有的公共交通。

4. it is constituted改为it constitutes

【译文】健康地理学领域经常被忽视，但它实际上是地理学和医疗保健领域中一块巨大的需求。

5. it was seemed改为it seemed

【译文】的确,在20世纪的最后几十年里,似乎任何东西都可以变成商品。

6. has long associated改为has long been associated

【译文】首先,它长久以来都与高质量产品联系在一起,它的传统形象与该类产品更相称。

7. C

【译文】样品房通常由大型项目建筑商提供,他们的工程规模大,可以提供良好的质量和划算的价格。

8. This is required改为This requires

【译文】这需要了解在不同的管理层面和不同的职业阶段是什么在激励员工。

9. C

【译文】有一种观点认为,探索太空是浪费金钱,地球上有更紧迫的需求需要解决,比如减少贫困和防止环境破坏。

10. born改为are born

【译文】虽然有证据表明,有些婴儿天生带有更容易犯罪的基因,但最终每个人都有决定是否违法的权力。

Exercise 4

1. More papers on the subject **have been published** since 2013.

2. Types of food **are** now freely **distributed to** every corner of the globe.

3. However, many non-biodegradable consumer goods **can be recycled** and potentially **reused** in other consumer goods.

4. Reading and writing on a mobile phone or tablet computer **is regarded** by many young people as faster and more convenient.

5. **It can be observed that** India, Indonesia and China had a higher percentage of dependants than the world average.

6. I still insist that teachers take on a role so important in education that it should not **be ignored**.

7. There is evidence to suggest that individuals are prone to **be** negatively **affected** by the advertisements they see.

8. Noticeably, the road bridge **was** dominantly **used** by private cars and public transport in 1965.

9. **It has been suggested that** the best way to decrease the death roll and improve road safety is to raise the minimum age for obtaining a driving licence.

10. Although other anti-social behaviours such as smoking **are** now **prohibited** in the majority of public spaces, I believe that people should be free to use their phones in public without restriction.

第3章　　如何使句子出彩

第1节　使用多变的句式

Exercise 1

1. Apart from

【译文】除犯罪调查技术外,学生们还学习法医学、哲学和逻辑学。

【解析】criminal investigation techniques和forensic medicine、philosophy、logic之间是并列且互不包含的关系,故选Apart from"除了……外(还)"。Due to意为"由于"。

2. In order to

【译文】为了最大限度地增加利润,这家公司将试图最大限度地增加产量。

【解析】maximize profit使用了动词原形,而且是to maximize output的目的,故选In order to"为了"。In addition to意为"除了……外(还)"。

3. Thanks to

【译文】由于有了汽车,美国人很快就获得了前所未有的行动自由。

【解析】automobile是令美国人获得行动自由的原因,故选Thanks to"幸亏,由于"。In case of意为"如果发生,假使"。

4. Despite

【译文】尽管采取了这些措施，经济仍然停滞不前。

【解析】前后语句之间是转折关系，故选 Despite "尽管"。Besides 意为"除了……外(还)"。

5. Geographically

【译文】从地理上看，女性预期寿命最低的县位于阿巴拉契亚地区和南部地区。

【解析】空格所填的词放在开头，用于修饰全句，限定讨论角度，故应选副词 Geographically "从地理上看"。Geographical 意为"地理的，地理位置的"。

6. Unfortunately

【译文】遗憾的是，几乎没有可能看到这些重大问题得到解答。

【解析】空格要填入的为评述性状语，修饰整个句子，表示作者对句子内容的看法。根据句意，重大问题得不到解答应该是一件遗憾的事，故选 Unfortunately。Suddenly 意为"突然"。

Exercise 2

1. There are disadvantages to the plan.

【译文】这个计划有诸多弊端。

2. There seem to be fewer tourists around this year.

【译文】今年周围的游客似乎减少了。

3. So well *did they succeed* **that** by 2010 they were forced to reverse course.

【译文】他们(的政策)太奏效，以至于到 2010 年，他们被迫改变了方向。

4. Only when the shareholder actually sells his own shares *does a taxable event occur*.

【译文】只有当股东实际出售他自己的股票时才会产生应税事项。

5. Not only *are mothers not paid* **but** most of their boring or difficult work is also unnoticed.

【译文】母亲们不仅得不到报酬，而且所干的乏味艰辛的活儿也很少被注意到。

Exercise 3

1. 强调部分: reason

【译文】那正是他感到有点痛苦的原因。

2. 强调部分: money

【译文】对竞选活动来说最重要的是钱。

3. 强调部分: the picture itself

【译文】是这张图片本身的问题。

4. 强调部分: not until after the second world war

【译文】直到第二次世界大战后，才出现了解释的雏形。

5. 强调部分: they

【译文】是他们需要开始做出让步——让自己活，也让别人活。

Exercise 4

1. It is important to understand the powerful economic and social forces at work behind our own actions.

2. It is clear that the primary duty of parents is to provide protection for their children.

3. It takes time for analysts and investors **to** fully digest a report and reassess expectations.

4. They **would have to learn** patience **if** they **were to get through** this.

5. It is high time we **started** being intellectually honest about all the failures in this country.

第2节 同义改写句子

Exercise 1

1. 替换词: Youngsters/The youth/Adolescents

【译文】年轻人常常违反规定。

2. 替换词: schooling

【译文】他对教育的看法不同寻常。

3. 替换词: merit/superiority/virtue

【译文】小型轿车还有一个优点是使用成本比较便宜。

4. 替换词: recreation/activity/amusement

【译文】在法国，下馆子是全国人普遍的消遣活动。

5. 替换词: resolve/address/tackle/cope with/deal with

【译文】他们能受托解决重大国家问题。

6. 替换词: support/stimulate

【译文】对孩子表达自我的尝试，你应当加以鼓励。

7. 替换词: astonishing/unusual/strange

【译文】孩子们学习阅读的速度不同并不奇怪。

8. 替换词: improve/promote

【译文】这是提高公司声誉的机会。

9. 替换词: active/positive

【译文】政府应该解决相关的污染和住房问题，这是消除可预防疾病更为积极的方法。

10. 替换词: extravagant/overmuch/superabundant/unrestrained

【译文】许多人把不断上升的暴力犯罪率归咎于电视节目和电影中过多的暴力镜头，因此政府应该对这些媒体的内容进行审查。

Exercise 2

1. invention

【译文】那项发明已经由那所大学获取了专利。

2. realisation

【译文】越来越多的人意识到变革势在必行。

3. flexibility

【译文】利用计算机，工作安排可以灵活得多。

4. responsibility

【译文】这个部门拒绝为所发生的事承担责任。

5. improvement

【译文】已经有了显著的改善。

6. Prior

【译文】在国内影院上映之前，中国所有的电影剧本都必须得到国家广播电视总局的审批。

7. evident

【译文】随着环境破坏问题愈发明显且广为人知，每一个人，不管身在何处，都在为拯救地球尽一份责任。

Exercise 3

1. 改写: As is shown in the table, American workers have very good reason to be afraid.

【译文】数据显示，美国工人有充分的理由感到害怕。

2. 改写: People believe that using electronic devices to communicate makes us lose the ability to communicate with each other face to face.

【译文】人们认为使用电子设备交流使我们失去了面对面交流的能力。

3. 改写: The government should control the amount of media/fictional violence in order to decrease violent crimes in society.

【译文】为了减少社会暴力犯罪，政府应该控制媒体中的暴力/虚拟暴力的数量。

4. 改写: Many traditional customs like female circumcision and arranged marriage are no longer relevant to the modern life and not worth keeping.

【译文】许多传统习俗，如女性割礼和包办婚姻，已不再适应现代生活，它们是不值得保留的。

5. 改写: Some people think that environmental problems like water pollution, air pollution and desertification are too big for individuals to solve. Others, however, believe that the problems cannot be solved if individuals do not take actions.

【译文】一些人认为，水污染、空气污染、荒漠化等环境问题非常严重，是个体无法解决的。然而，其他人则认为，只有个人采取行动，这些问题才能得以解决。

第3节 常用的论证句型

Exercise 1

1. due to

【译文】由于住房紧张，很多人买不起自己的房子。

【解析】空格后面是原因，故选due to。

2. as a result of

【译文】他们的身体因营养不良而扭曲变形。

【解析】空格后面是原因，故选as a result of。

3. because

【译文】被动的、枯燥的活动最有利于创造力的发挥，因为它可以让人的思想游离。

【解析】空格后面是原因，故选because。

4. so

【译文】斯堪的纳维亚地区气候一旦转冷很可能意味着大范围的作物歉收，因此更多人将依靠狩猎来弥补这些损失。

【解析】空格后面是结果,故选so。

5. thanks to

【译文】在野外,蚂蚁可能活不过140天,这要归因于捕食者、疾病以及比舒适的实验室恶劣得多的环境。

【解析】空格后面是原因,故选thanks to。

6. owing to

【译文】由于大衰退的特殊情况,他需要更多时间。

【解析】空格后面是原因,故选owing to。

7. resulting in

【译文】具有有限自驾能力的车辆已经存在了50多年,从而为驾驶辅助系统做出了重大贡献。

【解析】空格后面是结果,故选resulting in。

8. hence

【译文】我们怀疑他们试图隐瞒某些事情,因此有必要进行独立调查。

【解析】空格后面是结果,故选hence。

9. thus

【译文】大学扩招了,从而使更多的人有机会接受高等教育。

【解析】空格后面是结果,故选thus。

10. consequently

【译文】首先,缺乏信息流,从而导致建议质量下降。

【解析】空格后面是结果,故选consequently。

Exercise 2

1. **If** we want AI to really benefit people, we need to find a way to get people to trust it.

【译文】如果我们想让人工智能真正造福于人,我们需要找到一种方法让人们信任它。

2. Students are not allowed to handle these chemicals **unless** they are under the supervision of a teacher.

【译文】除非是在老师的监督下,否则学生不允许触碰这些化学品。

3. Mobility demand can be met by far fewer vehicles **if** a significant proportion of the population choose to use shared automated vehicles.

【译文】如果很大一部分人选择使用共享的自动驾驶车辆,就可以用更少的车辆来满足出行需求。

4. Individuals cannot solve these environmental problems **unless** governments take some actions.

【译文】除非政府采取行动,否则个人无法解决这些环境问题。

5. It is impossible for children to succeed at school **unless** they have help from their parents.

【译文】除非得到父母的帮助,否则孩子不可能在学校取得成功。

Exercise 3

1. 在other music sites前加that of

【译文】NPR广播的受众会比其他音乐网站的受众更广泛。

【解析】比较句中进行比较的是"NPR广播的受众"和"其他音乐网站的受众",比较对象需一致。根据主句的谓语动词tends使用了第三人称单数形式可知,此处audience为单数名词,故用that指代。

2. 在any other primate前加those of

【译文】人类幼儿依赖成年人的时间比其他任何灵长类动物的幼崽都要长得多。

【解析】比较句中进行比较的是"人类的幼儿"和"其他任何灵长类动物的幼崽",比较对象需一致。children是可数名词复数,所以用those指代。

3. good at改为better at

【译文】我们生活中的许多决定都需要好的预测,而人工智能几乎总是比我们更擅长预测。

【解析】这句是"比较级+than"的用法,than前面的形容词good应该用比较级better。

4. more改为much

【译文】他带我们进入微生物的世界,试图说服我们像他一样爱它们。

【解析】as… as表示"像……一样",两个as中间应该用形容词或副词的原形,因此应该将more改为much,修饰动词love。

5. much改为more

【译文】琼斯负伤以来,与其说他是全队的骨干倒不如说他已成为队里的累赘。

【解析】这里是"more of a/an+名词+than"的句型，意为"与其说……不如说……"，因此应为more of a liability than an asset。

Exercise 4

1. The introduction of driverless vehicles will **result in** greater safety.

2. Recycling also reduces the need for raw materials to be quarried, **thus** saving precious resources.

3. **For this reason**, bilingual people often perform better on tasks that require conflict management.

4. There are hundreds of channels, and **therefore** you can always find something that is worth watching.

5. **If** the soil loses its ability to perform these functions, the human race could be in big trouble.

6. He agreed to speak to reporters **on condition that** he was not identified.

7. Recovery can't be sustained **unless** more jobs are created.

8. Cats sleep twice **as much as** people do.

9. Many caged birds live **longer than** their fellows in the wild.

10. Ebola is **not as** easily spread **as** viruses such as smallpox.

第4章 写作综合训练 250 句

第1节 基础训练150句

Exercise 1

1. have改为has

【译文】我们每个人都需要在促进社区的平等和社会正义方面发挥作用。

【考点】主谓一致

【解析】each表示"每一"，是单数概念，each of...结构作主语，谓语动词用单数。

2. were改为was

【译文】在18世纪，美术和音乐、诗歌一样被看作是具有启迪作用的。

【考点】主谓一致

【解析】along with music and poetry可以被看作是插入语，主语是art，谓语动词用单数。

3. aim counteract改为aim to counteract

【译文】这些训练旨在抵消压力与紧张的影响。

【考点】非谓语动词

【解析】aim to do sth.意为"打算做某事，力求做某事"，是固定搭配。

4. Read改为Reading

【译文】阅读这篇短文很有启发。

【考点】非谓语动词

【解析】谓语动词不能直接作主语，因此需要把Read改成动名词Reading。

5. avoid to expend改为avoid expending

【译文】实际上，许多人都会千方百计地节省时间，避免耗费这一宝贵财富。

【考点】非谓语动词

【解析】avoid doing sth.意为"避免做某事"，是固定搭配。

6. having改为to have

【译文】大学生背负银行贷款已不足为奇。

【考点】非谓语动词

【解析】这里考查的是"It is+形容词+for sb.+to do sth."的句型，意为"某人做某事是……的"。

7. how coping改为how to cope

【译文】好像动物们不知道如何应对它们新获得的自由。

【考点】非谓语动词

【解析】这里的"疑问词+to do"作动词know的宾语，how to do sth.意为"如何做某事"。

8. without to leave改为without leaving

【译文】人们喜欢这个工具，因为他们可以在不离开家的情况下参加市政厅会议。

【考点】介词、非谓语动词

【解析】without是介词，后面的动词需要变成动名词形式。

9. travel改为travels

　【译文】如今消息传播得很快。

　【考点】可数名词与不可数名词

　【解析】news意为"新闻"，是不可数名词，谓语动词用单数。

10. photoes改为photos

　【译文】评论家和公众苦思冥想，想出了他照片中的层层含意。

　【考点】可数名词与不可数名词

　【解析】photo是可数名词，复数形式直接加-s。

11. informations改为information；were改为was

　【译文】此信息不易分类。

　【考点】可数名词与不可数名词

　【解析】information是不可数名词，不能加-s，谓语动词用单数。

12. This改为These

　【译文】最近的这些发现表明，许多货物在陆路上运输。

　【考点】限定词

　【解析】discoveries是名词复数，指示代词需相应用复数的these，表示"这些"。

13. a few改为a little

　【译文】这项新研究增加了一些证据，有助于决定平衡应该在哪里。

　【考点】限定词

　【解析】evidence是不可数名词，要用a little修饰。

14. solutions改为solution

　【译文】另一种解决方案也许是揭露更多关于人工智能使用的算法及算法目的的信息。

　【考点】限定词

　【解析】another表示"另一"，是单数含义，后面常接可数名词单数。

15. since改为for

　【译文】我们已经运行这个项目十年了，我们不希望改变其基本技术。

　【考点】介词

　【解析】for后面接时间段，since后面接时间点。

16. in改为to

　【译文】课程从烹饪到计算机技术都有。

　【考点】介词

　【解析】range from... to...意为"包括(各种不同的人或物)"，是固定搭配。

17. strive with改为strive for

　【译文】所有的努力都是为了人与自然之间、人们彼此之间的平衡、和谐与团结而奋斗。

　【考点】介词

　【解析】strive for意为"为……奋斗"，是固定搭配。

18. commit in改为commit to

　【译文】典型的问题是一旦复苏的苗头出现，中央银行是否能够做出维持通胀的可靠保证。

　【考点】介词

　【解析】commit to doing sth.意为"承诺做某事"，是固定搭配。

19. responsible in改为responsible for

　【译文】停车场所有者应该依法负责保护车辆。

　【考点】介词

　【解析】be responsible for意为"对……负责"，是固定搭配。

20. from改为of

　【译文】俱乐部可能会因为这一举动而被扣10分。

　【考点】介词

　【解析】as a result of表示"由于"，是固定搭配，后面接原因。

21. 删去Although或but

　【译文】尽管它们贵，但它们能一直用下去并且永不过时。

　【考点】连词

　【解析】英语中although和but不能同时使用。

22. and改为or

　【译文】观光最好乘坐游览巴士，要么骑自行车。

　【考点】连词

　【解析】either... or意为"或者……或者……"，表示选择。

23. or technology改为nor technology

　【译文】五年前，无论是创业还是技术，都不像如今这样酷炫，也没有那么受欢迎。

　【考点】连词

　【解析】neither... nor意为"既不……也不……"。

24. 删去Because或so

　【译文】由于是互联网和电子商务所用的语言，英语因此成为国际语言。

【考点】连词

【解析】英语中because和so不能同时使用。

25. so改为but

【译文】科学家已经研究了蜜蜂一些类似的方面，但最近关于蜜蜂的研究结果是混杂的。

【考点】连词

【解析】句子前后为转折关系，连词用but。

26. increasing改为increasingly

【译文】随着技术变得越来越复杂，在计算机艺术中找到更深层次的东西便成为可能。

【考点】副词

【解析】修饰形容词complex要用副词increasingly。

27. sharp改为sharply

【译文】总体而言，由于供应减少和需求增加，油价大幅上涨。

【考点】副词

【解析】修饰动词has increased要用副词sharply。

28. Admitted改为Admittedly

【译文】诚然，页岩占了整体工业生产增长18.3%的五分之一。

【考点】副词

【解析】副词admittedly意为"诚然，公认地"，修饰整个句子。

29. which改为whose

【译文】所有这些都是有益的品种，其潜力尚未被认识到。

【考点】定语从句

【解析】whose引导定语从句，指代所属关系，whose potentiality即potentiality of the useful breeds。

30. which改为where或者on/at which

【译文】有些人说，我们已经到了技术侵入我们私人生活的阶段。

【考点】定语从句

【解析】point在这里意思是"(发展)阶段，程度，地步"，在从句中作地点状语，表示"在这个阶段"，故关系词用where或on/at which。

31. that may help改为which may help

【译文】其他研究表明，将狗作为宠物饲养可以

让儿童尽早接触各种细菌，这可能有助于保护他们以后不会出现过敏。

【考点】定语从句

【解析】引导非限制性定语从句不能用that，此处关系词指代前一分句所说的事情，故用which。

32. in which改为with which

【译文】许多犯罪，如身份盗窃，是由于犯罪分子可以轻易在网上匿名操作造成的。

【考点】定语从句

【解析】该从句是"介词+which"引导的定语从句，修饰先行词the ease。表示"轻易"时，与ease搭配的介词用with，所以把in改为with。

33. which改为that

【译文】任何更方便供应商分享其设计的东西都将节省时间和金钱。

【考点】定语从句

【解析】先行词是不定代词anything时，定语从句用that引导。

34. that改为what

【译文】如果给予平等的机会，人们会因自己所取得的成就而得到相应的奖励。

【考点】宾语从句

【解析】介词for后需接宾语，而宾语从句中的及物动词accomplish后缺宾语，故用what引导宾语从句。

35. How改为What

【译文】他们提供的是最低价的优质产品。

【考点】主语从句

【解析】主语从句中的offer是及物动词，后面缺宾语，故用what引导。

36. if改为whether

【译文】一个重要的问题是，银行是否会在发挥监督的作用之外，提供经济援助。

【考点】表语从句

【解析】表示"是否"时，只能用whether引导表语从句，不能用if。

37. such改为so

【译文】的确，许多深受犯罪影响的受害人认为预防犯罪是注定要失败的。

【考点】状语从句

【解析】so... that 用于修饰形容词或副词, such...
　　　　that 用于修饰名词, severely 是副词, 故用
　　　　so... that 句型。

38. such 改为 so
【译文】房价如此之高, 以至于大多数人无法负
　　　　担住在靠近海岸的地方。
【考点】状语从句
【解析】so... that 用于修饰形容词或副词, such...
　　　　that 用于修饰名词, high 是形容词, 故用
　　　　so... that 句型。

39. will be 改为 is
【译文】磁盘如果过载, 数据就会出错。
【考点】状语从句
【解析】此句包含 if 引导的真实条件状语从句, 主句
　　　　用一般将来时, 从句用一般现在时, 即 "主
　　　　将从现"。

40. use 改为 be used
【译文】未来, 计算机将被用来制造更大、更复杂
　　　　的计算机。
【考点】被动语态
【解析】主语 computers 和动词 use 是被动关系, 因
　　　　此用被动语态。be used to do sth. 表示 "被
　　　　用来做某事"。

41. were taken place 改为 took place
【译文】这两幅地图描述了在1990年至2010年期
　　　　间某博物馆及其周边环境发生的变化。
【考点】被动语态
【解析】take place 意为 "发生", 是不及物动词, 没
　　　　有被动语态。

42. crime will disappear 改为 will crime disappear
【译文】只有消除更广泛的社会问题, 如贫困和
　　　　不平等, 犯罪活动才会消失。
【考点】倒装句
【解析】only 引导状语从句放在句首时, 主句要用
　　　　部分倒装结构。

43. No sooner the video was up 改为 No sooner
　　　was the video up
【译文】视频一上线, 全世界就有成千上万的人
　　　　想要观看。
【考点】倒装句

【解析】no sooner... than 意为 "一……就", 此时
　　　　no sooner 之后的从句要进行部分倒装。

44. which 改为 that
【译文】只有实现这些目标才会最终带来持久的
　　　　和平。
【考点】强调句
【解析】这是一个强调句, 强调部分为 only the
　　　　achievement of these goals, 指物, 引导
　　　　词只能用 that。

45. apprehended 改为 (should) apprehend
【译文】当地人要求警方逮捕那些歹徒。
【考点】虚拟语气
【解析】在动词 demand "要求" 后面的宾语从句, 谓
　　　　语用 "should+ 动词原形" 的虚拟语气结构,
　　　　should 可省略。

46. pay 改为 paid 或 should pay
【译文】现在是制造危机的人为此付出代价的时
　　　　候了。
【考点】虚拟语气
【解析】It is (high) time that 表示 "是该做……的
　　　　时候了", 从句谓语用过去式或 "should+ 动
　　　　词原形" 的虚拟语气结构, 注意其中 should
　　　　不可省略。

47. result from 改为 result in
【译文】竞争可以是良性的, 但如果被推向极端,
　　　　就会导致恃强凌弱。
【考点】因果句
【解析】result in 表示 "导致", 后面接结果; result
　　　　from 表示 "由……引起", 后面接原因。

48. fast 改为 faster
【译文】数字经济的增长速度是其他经济类型增
　　　　长速度的七倍。
【考点】比较句
【解析】句中出现 than, 是比较句, 副词 fast 应该用
　　　　比较级 faster。

49. that of 改为 those of
【译文】密密麻麻的行人造成的交通负荷可能比
　　　　乘用车造成的交通负荷重。
【考点】比较句
【解析】这句比较的是 pedestrian traffic loads
　　　　"行人造成的交通负荷" 和 traffic loads

of passenger cars "乘用车造成的交通负荷",为避免重复,故用those替代前面的复数名词traffic loads。

50. smoother改为smooth

【译文】通往阳光清洁的未来的道路并不像看起来那么平坦。

【考点】比较句

【解析】(not) as... as意为"(不)像……一样",两个as中间使用形容词或副词的原级。

Exercise 2

1. I think universities should provide theoretical knowledge **and** incorporate practical skills into the curriculum.

【译文】我认为大学应当在传授理论知识的同时,在课程中加入实用技能。

【解析】and连接两个分句,表并列关系。

2. Transportation is estimated to account for 30% of energy consumption in most of the world's most developed nations, **so** lowering the need for energy-using vehicles is essential for decreasing the environmental impact of mobility.

【译文】据估计,在世界上大多数最发达的国家中,交通占能源消耗的30%,因此降低对耗能车辆的需求对于减少交通对环境的影响至关重要。

【解析】so连接两个分句,表因果关系。

3. We might associate wisdom with intelligence or particular personality traits, **but** research shows only a small positive relationship between wise thinking and crystallised intelligence and the personality traits of openness and agreeableness.

【译文】我们可能会将智慧与智力或特定的人格特质联系起来,但研究表明,明智的思维和具象智力之间只存在很小的正相关关系,与开放友善的人格特质之间的关系也是如此。

【解析】but连接两个分句,表转折关系。

4. The awareness of competition could also serve as a positive factor in enhancing personal skills **such as** time management and communication.

【译文】竞争意识也能对提高时间管理和沟通等个人技能起到积极作用。

【解析】such as意为"例如",后面接例子。

5. I insist that teachers take on a role **so** important in education **that** it should not be ignored.

【译文】我坚持认为,教师在教育中扮演的角色至关重要,不容忽视。

【解析】so... that意为"如此……以至于……",so是副词,在这里用来修饰形容词important,that引导结果状语从句。

6. The product was **such** a hit **that** women wore them as accessories around concert grounds.

【译文】该产品很受欢迎,以至于女性在音乐会将它们作为配饰佩戴。

【解析】such... that意为"如此……以至于……",such后面接名词,that引导结果状语从句。

7. **Although** certain aspects of parenting may come naturally, I agree that taking a parenting course can benefit both parents and children.

【译文】尽管某些育儿技巧也许是自然而然就会的,但我认为参加育儿课程对父母和孩子都有益。

【解析】although意为"虽然,尽管",用于引导让步状语从句。

8. We possess both the science and the technology to identify and redress the changes in how we read **before** they become entrenched.

【译文】我们拥有科学和技术来识别和改正我们阅读方式的变化,以免它们变得根深蒂固。

【解析】before在此句中意为"以免,免得",用于引导时间状语从句。

9. An individual might go to McDonald's and purchase five Big Mac burgers after seeing an advertisement for Big Macs on television earlier that day.

【译文】某人可能在电视上看到巨无霸汉堡的广告后,就去麦当劳买五个巨无霸汉堡来吃。

【解析】after意为"在……之后",用于引导时间状语。

10. **While** laws may be needed to boost the amount of recycling, I believe that educating residents is much more important and a better way to achieve the same outcome.

【译文】虽然可能需要法律来提高回收量，但我认为，教育居民更为重要，也是取得同样效果的更好方法。

【解析】while意为"虽然，尽管"，用于引导让步状语从句。

11. The economy is in danger of collapse **unless** far-reaching reforms are implemented.

【译文】除非实施影响深远的改革，否则经济就有崩溃的危险。

【解析】unless意为"除非"，用于引导条件状语从句。

12. Actually, art classes provide a distraction, **allowing** our students a break from their intense study and constant competition.

【译文】实际上，艺术课提供了一种消遣，让我们的学生从紧张的学习和无休止的竞争中放松片刻。

【解析】现在分词allowing引导的短语在句中作方式状语。

13. Another disadvantage of always trying to outstrip others is mental problems **resulting** from constant pressure.

【译文】总是试图超越他人带来的另一个弊端是持续的压力会导致心理问题。

【解析】现在分词resulting引导的短语在句中作后置定语，修饰mental problems。

14. **Seen** from afar, the towering buildings beckon the visitor in.

【译文】远远望去，那些高耸建筑就像在召唤游客。

【解析】过去分词Seen引导的短语在句中作状语。

15. **Travelling** around Thailand in the 1990s, William Janssen was impressed with the basic rooftop solar heating systems that were on many homes.

【译文】20世纪90年代，威廉·詹森在泰国各地旅行，对许多家庭屋顶上的基础太阳能加热系统印象深刻。

【解析】现在分词Travelling引导的短语在句中作状语。

16. **Having learned** a lesson, we reacted.

【译文】吸取了教训后，我们做出了反应。

【解析】Having learned是现在分词的完成式，引导的短语在句中作状语。

17. Dads didn't raise their pitch or fundamental frequency **when** they talked to kids.

【译文】爸爸在与孩子交谈时不会提高他们的音调或基本频率。

【解析】when意为"当……时"，引导时间状语从句。

18. We should adapt ourselves to it **rather than** prevent it.

【译文】我们应该适应它，而不是阻止它。

【解析】rather than意为"与其……宁可……"，连接两个平行的结构。

19. The fear of losing job security is often **so** strong **that** it essentially paralyses people to the point of settling for mediocrity and never venturing outside of their comfort zone.

【译文】对失去工作保障的恐惧往往是如此强烈，以至于它从根本上麻痹人们安于平庸，永远不敢走出自己的舒适区。

【解析】so... that意为"如此……以至于……"，引导结果状语从句。

20. **Despite the fact that** almost all agencies have the same basic capabilities, their creative standards differ.

【译文】尽管几乎所有机构都具有相同的基本能力，但它们的创意标准却不同。

【解析】despite the fact that意为"尽管"，后面接fact的同位语从句。

21. Children do **not** learn to walk **until** their bodies are ready.

【译文】身体准备好的时候，小孩子才会学走路。

【解析】not... until意为"直到……才"，引导时间状语从句。

22. There were around 550,000 visitors in the Natural History Museum, **whereas** 400,000 visitors went to the Science Museum.

【译文】自然历史博物馆的参观者约为55万人，而科学博物馆的参观者为40万人。

【解析】whereas意为"然而，但是"，用以比较、对比两个事实。

23. Theoretical knowledge prepares us for further education, **which** is essential since lifelong learning is more necessary than ever in this ever-evolving society.

【译文】理论知识让我们为进一步的教育做好准备，这很重要，因为在这个不断发展的社会中，终身学习比以往任何时候都更有必要。

【解析】关系代词which引导非限制性定语从句，指代前面整个主句的内容。

24. Childcare centres exist to ensure the safety and well-being of the young children **who** have not yet commenced their primary school education.

【译文】育儿中心的出现是为了确保那些尚未上小学的幼儿的安全和健康。

【解析】先行词young children是人，用关系代词who引导定语从句。

25. People eat **when** they are depressed.

【译文】人们会在沮丧时吃东西。

【解析】when意为"当……时"，引导时间状语从句。

26. Needless to say, this necessitates a long-term commitment to countless hours of hard work, **which** requires steadfast determination.

【译文】不用说，这需要保证长期不断勤奋工作，因此要有坚定的决心。

【解析】后一个句子是对commitment的补充说明，因此可以转换为which引导的非限制性定语从句，修饰前一句的commitment。

27. If two different goods have the same price, it can be claimed that they produce the same quantity of pleasure in the consumer.

【译文】如果两种不同的商品具有相同的价格，则可以声称它们为消费者提供同样多的愉悦感。

【解析】if意为"如果"，引导条件状语从句。

28. As global temperatures continue to rise, we are going to continue to squander more and more energy on keeping our buildings mechanically cool **until** we have run out of capacity.

【译文】随着全球气温持续上升，我们将继续浪费越来越多的能源对建筑物持续进行物理降温，直到我们将能源用尽。

【解析】until意为"直到……"，引导时间状语从句。

29. **If** a government wants to preserve and maintain the art and music **which** are historically traditional to the country, it must take steps to ensure that those traditions are valued and fostered.

【译文】政府如果想保存和维护其国家历史上传统的艺术和音乐，就必须采取措施确保这些传统得到重视和发扬。

【解析】if意为"如果"，引导条件状语从句。which引导限制性定语从句，修饰先行词the art and music。

30. Here I am referring to the print newspaper, **whose** readership is indeed steadily declining in the past decade.

【译文】这里我指的是纸质报纸，其读者人数在过去十年里确实在稳步下降。

【解析】whose引导定语从句，表示"……的"。在此句中，whose readership指的是the print newspaper's readership，也就是"纸质报纸的读者人数"。

31. People **who** travel on the underground don't carry their bikes around.

【译文】乘坐地铁出行的人不会随身携带自行车。

【解析】用who引导限制性定语从句，修饰先行词People。

32. Older parents generally have less stressed about income or job security **so that** they tend to be more patient and can spend more time with their children.

【译文】年龄较大的父母收入压力更小，工作也更有保障，这样他们更有耐心，有更多时间陪伴孩子。

【解析】so that意为"所以,结果",引导结果状语从句。

33. **As long as** the culture remains intact, the team will eventually find its success.

【译文】只要文化保持不变,团队最终将会获得成功。

【解析】as long as意为"只要",引导条件状语从句。

34. Our stories were not the same, **yet** I found myself in each one of them.

【译文】我们的故事各不相同,然而我在每一个故事中都找到了自己。

【解析】yet意为"然而,可是",表转折关系。

35. Women are looking for career development **as well as** making a contribution to the nation.

【译文】妇女正在寻求职业发展,同时为国家做出贡献。

【解析】as well as意为"也,又"。两个句子的主语都是Women,可以用as well as并列两个动宾结构。

36. **Even if** access to information and knowledge is much easier today than in the past, I still insist that teachers take on a role so important in education that it should not be ignored.

【译文】即使在今天获取信息和知识比过去简单得多,我仍然坚持认为教师在教育中扮演的角色至关重要,不容忽视。

【解析】even if意为"即使",引导让步状语从句。

37. This is an important step **not only** to ensure what is learned is useful **but also** to prevent students from accessing information that would produce deleterious effects on their mentality.

【译文】这一步很重要,因为不仅能确保学生学到有用的东西,还能防止他们接触到那些会毒害心灵的信息。

【解析】not only... but also意为"不仅……而且……",用于连接两个并列的成分,着重强调后者。

38. The website was set up to allow **both** individuals **and** travel organisations to create itineraries and travel packages to suit their own needs and interests.

【译文】该网站的建立是为了让个人和旅行机构根据自己的需求和兴趣创建行程和旅行套餐。

【解析】both... and意为"两者都……",连接两个对等的成分。

39. You can **either** try to dance to it **or** try to escape it as much as possible.

【译文】你可以试着随着它起舞,或者尽可能地摆脱它。

【解析】either... or意为"或者……或者……",表示两者选其一,连接两个并列的成分。

40. The majority of workers work unofficially with **neither** health insurance **nor** wage security.

【译文】大多数工人是非正式的工作关系,既没有健康保险,也没有工资保障。

【解析】neither... nor意为"既不……也不……",其含义是否定的,连接两个并列的成分。

41. Today's editions are likely to survive in large quantities **thanks to** more durable materials.

【译文】多亏了更耐用的材料,如今的版本有可能大量留存下来。

【解析】thanks to意为"由于,多亏",后面接名词表示原因。

42. It is a very hopeful principle when applied to critical thought in the reading brain **because** it implies choice.

【译文】当这条原则应用于阅读大脑的批判性思维时,我们看到了希望,因为它意味着还有选择。

【解析】because意为"因为",后面接从句表示原因。

43. Workers were later allowed back in **or** told to return by the factory owners.

【译文】工人后来被允许返回或被工厂主告知返回。

【解析】or意为"或者",表示其他可能性。

44. **As soon as** this mindset takes over, the potential for neglect, abuse, and even destruction of the local culture and environment will increase dramatically.

【译文】一旦这种心态占主导,那么忽略、滥用、甚至是破坏当地文化和环境的可能性就会急剧提高。

【解析】as soon as意为"一……就",引导时间状语从句。

45. They can come to the clinic **whenever** they want.

【译文】只要他们想来,他们可以随时到诊所来。

【解析】whenever意为"在任何……的时候",引导时间状语从句。

46. **Once** the project is completed, performances will increase, and museum opening hours will be extended.

【译文】项目一旦完成后,演出将增加,博物馆开放时间也将延长。

【解析】once意为"一旦……就",引导时间状语从句。

47. **Wherever** there is such demand for tropical agribusiness, forests are being razed to meet it.

【译文】无论何处,只要有热带农场经营的需求,森林就被摧毁以满足需求。

【解析】wherever意为"在任何地方",引导地点状语从句。

48. Their movements have been severely circumscribed **since** the laws came into effect.

【译文】自法律生效以来,他们的行动受到严重限制。

【解析】since意为"自从",引导时间状语从句。

49. **Provided that** these advancements continue to be informed by our collective humanity and desire for progress, the outlook is promising.

【译文】只要这些进步继续建立在我们的集体人性和对进步的渴望上,前景就很有希望。

【解析】provided that意为"如果,只要",引导条件状语从句。

50. **By the time** children reach the age of 15, this figure almost doubles to 18%.

【译文】到孩子年满15岁时,这个数字几乎翻了一番,达到18%。

【解析】by the time意为"到……的时候",引导时间状语从句。

Exercise 3

1. In the business world, **it is common for** company directors and managers **to be** older than other employees.

【译文】在商界,企业的董事和经理通常都会比其他员工年长。

【解析】"It+be+形容词+for sb. to do sth."意为"对某人来说做某事是……的"。

2. **It** generally **takes** many years of hard work and dedication **to be** promoted to the most senior positions within a company.

【译文】要晋升到一个企业最高级的职位通常需要多年的努力工作和奉献。

【解析】It takes... to do sth.意为"做某事需要花…… (时间、金钱等)"。

3. **It is** older people **who** are best suited to leadership roles due to their superior knowledge, experience and decision-making abilities.

【译文】因为年龄更大的人知识和经验更丰富,决策能力更强,所以他们是最合适的领导者人选。

【解析】当被强调的部分是人时,引导词可以用who或that。

4. **It is** the pressure **that** releases the coffee oils.

【译文】是压力将咖啡的油脂释放出来。

【解析】当被强调的部分是物时,引导词用that。

5. **It is** the inspection process itself **that** is likely to make the most difference.

【译文】检查过程本身可能带来最大的影响。

【解析】当被强调的部分是物时,引导词用that。

6. **Only when** a journalist is willing to do whatever it takes to uncover the truth and inform the public, **can they** start to build a reputation as a reliable and believable reporter.

【译文】只有当新闻记者愿意尽其所能发掘真相,并公之于众,他们才能开始树立声誉,成为可靠可信的记者。

【解析】"only when..., can+主语"意为"只有当……才能……",主句的情态动词can要提前,放在主语they的前面。

7. **It is believed by some people that** universities and colleges should teach practical subjects that are deemed more related to employment.

【译文】有人认为高等院校应当教授和就业更紧密相关的实用学科。

【解析】It is believed by sb. that...意为"某人认为……"。

8. **It has** long **been debated whether** art courses should be made a compulsory part of the curriculum at high school.

【译文】人们一直在争论是否应该将艺术课纳入高中的必修课程。

【解析】It is debated whether...意为"人们争论是否……"。

9. **It is claimed that** the construction process is faster, that waste is reduced and that there is less disruption to the environment.

【译文】据说，施工过程更快，废料减少，对环境的破坏也更小。

【解析】It is claimed that...意为"有人主张……，据说……"。

10. **It is suggested that** all the young adults should undertake a period of unpaid work helping people in the community.

【译文】有人建议所有年轻人都应当做一段时间的社区义工。

【解析】It is suggested that...意为"有人建议……"。

11. **Due to their lack of** driving experience, young drivers are more likely to adopt unsafe driving practices and fail to observe road hazards.

【译文】由于缺乏驾驶经验，年轻司机更有可能会有不安全的驾驶行为，不能观察到道路上的危险。

【解析】due to意为"由于，因为"，后面接名词，表示原因。one's lack of意为"某人在……方面的缺乏"，在此短语中lack是名词。

12. **Without** an honest disposition and strong moral principles to guide them, aspiring journalists will be destined for failure before they even begin their careers.

【译文】如果没有正直的性格和强大的道德准则作为指引，即使是胸怀大志的新闻记者也注定失败，甚至在职业生涯尚未开启时就败下阵来。

【解析】if there is not... 意为"如果没有……"，在这里可以用without改写，更为简洁。

13. As far as I am concerned, the government funding should not **be restricted to** the scholarship for the best students.

【译文】在我看来，政府的资金不应只局限用于为最优秀学生颁发奖学金。

【解析】be confined to 和 be restricted to 为同义短语，意为"被限制，局限于"。

14. Being innovative and creative **is beneficial to** problem-solving and prepares students for their future study.

【译文】富有革新意识和创造性有助于培养解决问题的能力，为学生的深造做好准备。

【解析】be good for 和 be beneficial to 为同义短语，意为"对……有好处"。

15. Despite the many benefits of volunteer work, there are some drawbacks that have a tendency to **deter** young people **from** getting involved.

【译文】尽管志愿工作有很多益处，但也存在一些弊端，往往会影响年轻人参与其中。

【解析】stop sb. from doing sth. 与 deter sb. from doing sth. 为同义搭配，意为"阻止某人做某事"。

16. The introduction of childcare centres **has sparked controversy** among working parents in recent years.

【译文】近年来育儿中心的出现在双职工父母中引起了争议。

【解析】spark controversy 意为"引起争议"。controversy 是名词，意为"争议"，controversial 是形容词，意为"有争议的"。

17. **Prior to** the availability of television sets, people would spend greater amounts of leisure time outdoors in the local community.

【译文】在电视机普遍使用之前，人们会花更多的时间在当地社区进行户外休闲活动。

【解析】prior to意为"在……之前",可与before互换。

18. As long as there are taxpayers to offset the high costs associated with free public healthcare, there is no reason why we cannot all **have access to** medical treatment if and when needed.

【译文】只要有纳税人来抵消免费公共医疗相关的高额费用,就没有理由让我们任何一个人在有需要的时候得不到医疗服务。

【解析】have access to意为"使用,接近",可与原句中的get互换。

19. **It is imperative that** governments control the water supply and enforce restrictions when and where necessary.

【译文】政府必须控制水资源的供给,同时在有必要的情况下加强监管。

【解析】It is imperative that...意为"……是非常重要的"。

20. **Despite** the efforts of worldwide cooperation, individuals remain the necessary driving force behind long-term, sustainable solutions.

【译文】尽管有全球性合作,个人仍然是长远的、可持续的解决方案背后的必要推动力。

【解析】despite意为"尽管",后接名词;而although引导让步状语时,其后接分句。

21. If democracy can work, then **so can** environmental action.

【译文】如果民主体制可行的话,那么环保行动也一样。

【解析】表示相同的情况对某物也适用时,可以用"so+助动词/be动词/情态动词+主语"的倒装结构,so意为"也,同样"。

22. **There has been a** significant **increase in** the number of single-person households.

【译文】独居人口的数量增长很快。

【解析】an increase in意为"在……方面的增长",在这里increase是名词。

23. **There has been a** profound **shift in** the social dynamics of local communities in recent years.

【译文】近年来地方社区的社会动态已经发生了深远的变革。

【解析】a shift in意为"在……方面的改变",在这里shift是名词。

24. Art **is** still **regarded by** the masses as an important form of creative expression.

【译文】艺术仍被大众视作创意表达的一种重要形式。

【解析】be regarded as... by sb.意为"被某人视为……"。

25. Since speeding and drink-driving offenders are not limited to the young driver age bracket, targeting these offences **as opposed to** targeting young drivers in general would have a greater impact on improving the overall level of road safety.

【译文】由于超速和酒后驾驶都不局限于年轻司机的范围,因此相对于针对普遍年轻司机,针对这些违规行为本身对提高总体的道路安全水平有更大的影响。

【解析】as opposed to意为"相对于、而非",表示对比,可与原句的instead of互换。需注意as opposed to后面接动词的doing形式。

26. **Regardless of** where we live in the world, we all tend to exist within a cultural bubble that reflects our surrounding environment and the people we interact with on a daily basis.

【译文】无论我们生活在世界上哪个地方,我们往往活在自身的文化泡沫中,这个泡沫反映着我们的周边环境和日常我们交往的人。

【解析】regardless of意为"不顾,不管",与原句中的No matter互换。

27. In my opinion, humanity should **endeavour to** preserve the world's remaining languages at all costs.

【译文】在我看来,人类应该不惜一切代价尽力去保护世界上留存的语言。

【解析】endeavour to do sth.意为"尽力做某事"，可与try one's best to do sth.互换。

28. Museums and historical sites **are** often **thought of** as tourism attractions rather than places of interest that appeal to tourists and locals alike.

【译文】博物馆和历史遗迹常常被看作是旅游景点，而不是对游客和当地人同样有吸引力的有趣的地方。

【解析】be thought of as意为"被认为是……"。

29. Vacation **is seen as** a time to relax, enjoy ourselves and do things that we would not normally do at home.

【译文】假期被看作是放松心情、享受生活的时候，我们会做一些在家一般不会做的事情。

【解析】be seen as意为"被看作是……"。

30. People **sitting at home** can research complicated issues with a few clicks of a mouse.

【译文】现在人们坐在家里只需点击几下鼠标即可研究复杂的问题。

【解析】现在分词短语sitting at home作后置定语，修饰主语People。

31. The crowd, **having been thin** for the first half of the race, had now grown considerably.

【译文】上半场比赛时观众稀稀拉拉的，现在则大大增多了。

【解析】现在分词短语having been thin for the first half of the race作后置定语，修饰The crowd。

32. Infrastructure is a major issue **continuing to affect millions of people**.

【译文】基础设施是持续影响数百万人的主要问题。

【解析】现在分词短语continuing to affect millions of people作后置定语，修饰a major issue。

33. Growers, **noticing this trend**, began growing more and more tulips with increasingly exotic sounding names and colours.

【译文】种植商注意到了这一趋势，开始种植越来越多的郁金香，名字和颜色也越来越奇特。

【解析】现在分词短语noticing this trend作伴随状语。

34. That means the stories **submitted by users** are not edited, fact-checked or screened before they post.

【译文】这意味着用户提交的故事在发布之前不会经过编辑、事实检查或筛选。

【解析】过去分词短语submitted by users作后置定语，修饰宾语从句的主语the stories。

35. Knitting offered people from poor communities a way of making extra money **while doing other tasks**.

【译文】针织为贫困社区的人们提供了一种在做其他任务的同时赚取额外收入的方式。

【解析】while doing sth.意为"当做某事的时候"，是"while sb.+be+doing sth."的省略形式。

36. Among the changes has been the first aid equipment, **owing to** advances in technology.

【译文】由于技术的进步，急救设备发生了变化。

【解析】owing to意为"由于，因为"，与because of一样，后面接名词，表示原因。

37. **The cause of** the crash was given as engine failure.

【译文】撞车事故的原因被认定是发动机故障。

【解析】the cause of和the reason for为同义短语，意为"……的原因"。

38. Damage may **result in** stunted growth and sometimes death of the plant.

【译文】损伤可能会导致植物生长受阻，有时还会导致死亡。

【解析】result in意为"导致"，后面接名词表示结果，与原句中的cause互换。

39. A poor diet will ultimately **lead to** illness.

【译文】糟糕的饮食最终会致病。

【解析】lead to意为"导致"，后面接名词表示结果，与原句中的result in互换。

40. **For this reason**, services have been drastically reduced.

【译文】结果,服务被大大减少了。

【解析】for this reason意为"结果",与原句中的 As a result互换。

41. **Consequently**, they were more likely to be influenced by the guesses that other people made.

【译文】因此,他们更有可能受到其他人的猜测的影响。

【解析】副词consequently意为"结果",与原句中的Therefore互换。

42. The other banks are going to be very eager to help, **on condition that** they see that he has a specific plan.

【译文】其他银行会非常渴望提供资助,只要它们看到他有一个具体的计划。

【解析】on condition that意为"如果,在……条件下",引导条件状语从句,与原句中的 provided that互换。

43. **As long as** there was enough land and the economy kept growing, there were few problems.

【译文】只要有足够的土地,并且经济持续增长,就几乎没有什么问题。

【解析】as long as意为"只要",引导条件状语从句,与原句中的So long as互换。

44. The theatre faces closure **unless** it gets an urgent cash injection.

【译文】剧院面临着倒闭,除非有救急现金投入。

【解析】unless意为"除非",与原句中的if... not互换。

45. People give various reasons and excuses for not recycling **on a regular basis**.

【译文】人们对于没能定期回收利用废品有各种各样的理由及借口。

【解析】on a regular basis意为"定期地,经常地",可与regularly互换。

46. The teacher should encourage the child to proceed **as far as he can**.

【译文】老师应当鼓励孩子尽可能地继续完成。

【解析】as... as sb. can意为"尽某人所能",与as... as possible同义。

47. The majority of people **place a high value on** their time and therefore resent the inconvenience of long commutes between frequented destinations, such as home, work, and school.

【译文】大多数人都非常珍视时间,因此会对经常去的地方,如家、公司和学校之间的长距离通勤所带来的不便感到不满。

【解析】place a high value on sth.意为"非常重视某物",可与原句中的highly value进行替换。

48. **Should you** be fired, your health and pension benefits would not be automatically cut off.

【译文】如果你失业了,你的医疗津贴和养老金将不会自动中断。

【解析】此句是对未来情况做假设的虚拟条件句,故可以把条件状语从句的If省略,should提前至主语you前,形成倒装。

49. **Were it** that simple, mothers would be defined by those things alone.

【译文】如果是那么简单,母亲们就会只被那些东西定义。

【解析】此句是对现在情况做假设的虚拟条件句,故可以把条件状语从句的If省略,were提前至主语it前,形成倒装。

50. **Had we** left the situation alone and done nothing, we would have been on the other side of it by now.

【译文】如果我们当初不理会局势,什么都不做,我们现在就会站在局势的另一边。

【解析】此句是对过去情况做假设的虚拟条件句,故可以把条件状语从句的If省略,had提前至主语we前,形成倒装。

Test 1

① sientists 改为 scientists；

　organizms 改为 organisms；

　agriculturul 改为 agricultural；

　medicanal 改为 medicinal

② ginetic 改为 genetic；

　medicanal 改为 medicinal；

　agriculturul 改为 agricultural

③ ethacal 改为 ethical；

　controvertial 改为 controversial

④ medacines 改为 medicines

⑤ dyeing 改为 dying；

　diseese 改为 disease；

　medacine 改为 medicine；

　treetment 改为 treatment；

　beleive 改为 believe

⑥ teckniques 改为 techniques；

　unethacal 改为 unethical；

　teckniques 改为 techniques；

　unnecesary 改为 unnecessary

⑧ preffer 改为 prefer

⑨ Naturaly 改为 Naturally；

　organnic 改为 organic；

　ocurring 改为 occurring

⑩ jeans 改为 genes

⑪ determuned 改为 determined

⑫ conclushion 改为 conclusion；

　modifickation 改为 modification；

　geanes 改为 genes；

　potenshially 改为 potentially

【译文】

　　①科学技术的新进展使科学家们能够开发出改变生物体生物构成的手段，从而改造农产品和医药产品。②显然，转基因技术有利也有弊，我个人认为，基因修改技术应该用来改造医药产品，而不应该改造农产品。

　　③与转基因技术相关的伦理和健康问题很多，这是一个复杂且极具争议性的问题。④我认为，当转基因技术被用于开发新药或有助于延长人类生命的科学技术时，它是有益的。⑤例如，如果一个人因患不治之症而生命垂危，而转基因技术可以提供一种新的药物或治疗方法，使这个人多活几年，那么我认为应该使用它。⑥然而，我认为像克隆这样的技术是不合乎伦理的，而且有潜在的危险，因为这些技术的作用是未知的，而且基本上没有必要。

　　⑦转基因技术也被用来改变农产品的生物特征。⑧例如，人们喜欢购买鲜黄色的香蕉，因为它们看起来新鲜健康。⑨然而，自然生长的有机香蕉并不是完美的黄色，相反，上面往往会自然形成一些由糖分引起的棕色斑点。⑩科学家们已经开发出改变香蕉基因的方法，以防止它们变成棕色。⑪在我看来，这种转基因技术是不必要的，而且可能使人们遭受不必要的风险，因为还不确定基因改变会带来什么样的健康风险。

　　⑫总之，基因修改技术应该用于必要和有用的目的，如拯救生命，而不是用于重新排列基因以改变农产品的外观，后者是一种具有潜在危险且不必要的做法。

Test 2

① **In** our modern, fast paced society, traditional food has often been replaced by fast food alternatives. ② **There** are advantages and disadvantages of both traditional and fast food meals, but **I** prefer traditional food because it is healthier, less expensive, and more enjoyable, to prepare, eat, and share.

③ **Fast** food has many advantages. ④ **Firstly,** fast food restaurants like **McDonald's** and **Burger King** are plentiful and provide **take-away** meals that can be consumed on the run, so busy individuals do not have to sacrifice valuable time to eat their meals. ⑤ **Pre-packaged** meals can also be prepared at home in minutes with little effort. ⑥ **However,** fast food also has its disadvantages. ⑦ **For** example, fast food is often expensive. ⑧ **Fast** food is frequently high in fat and salt, which, when consumed on a regular basis, can contribute to health problems like obesity and high blood pressure.

⑨ **Similarly**, traditional food also has advantages and disadvantages. ⑩ **The** advantages of traditional food preparation are that the ingredients of a traditional meal are often healthy, inexpensive, in season, and produced locally, sustaining local farmers and growers. ⑪ **The** seasonings added to traditional meals are usually varied and enrich the diet. ⑫ **One** of the disadvantages of traditional cooking is that it often takes time and careful effort. ⑬ **Some** people may view this as an advantage, however, because cooking skills are developed during this process and the ingredients are well savoured while related traditions such as dining etiquette and family gathering are promoted.

⑭ **In** my opinion, while fast food is convenient and easy, it is often unhealthy and expensive. ⑮ **Personally**, I prefer to spend a few extra minutes preparing a meal which is worth savouring and sharing than to indulge in expensive fast food meals that are greasy, salty and, in my opinion, unsatisfying.

【译文】
①在我们这个快节奏的现代社会中,传统食物常常被快餐所取代。②传统食物和快餐各有利弊,但我更喜欢传统食物,因为它更健康,更便宜,而且在烹饪、食用和分享时更让人感到愉快。

③快餐有很多优点。④首先,诸如麦当劳、汉堡王等快餐店很多,可以提供外卖让顾客在路上吃,所以忙碌的人不必牺牲宝贵的时间来吃饭。⑤预先包装好的饭菜在家里也可以不费吹灰之力,在几分钟内就做好。⑥然而,快餐也有缺点。⑦例如,快餐往往很贵。⑧快餐经常是高脂高盐食物,如果经常食用,会导致肥胖和高血压等健康问题。

⑨同样,传统食品也有优点和缺点。⑩制作传统食物的好处是,传统膳食的食材通常健康、平价、应季,并且是当地生产,维持了当地农民和种植户的生计。⑪添加到传统膳食中的调味品通常是多种多样的,丰富了饮食。⑫传统烹饪的缺点之一是,它往往很费时间,需要精心准备。⑬然而,有些人可能认为这是一个优点,因为在这个过程中烹饪技巧得到增进,食材被充分品尝,同时用餐礼仪和家人聚餐等相关传统得到宣扬。

⑭在我看来,快餐虽然方便简单,但它往往不健康且价格昂贵。⑮个人而言,我更愿意多花几分钟时间准备一顿值得品味和分享的饭菜,而不是沉迷于昂贵的快餐,这些快餐油腻而且太咸,在我看来不令人满意。

Test 3

①the	②a; the	③/
④the; the	⑤their	⑥/; the
⑦/; a	⑧the; the	⑨the; an
⑩many	⑪the; the	⑫their; the
⑬their		

【译文】
①世界上有数以千计的动物园,它们在全世界范围内饲养了数以百万计的动物。②许多人认为把动物关在笼子里是残忍和不自然的,但也有人认为,动物园可以保护动物,如果没有动物园,许多被饲养在动物园里面的动物将面临灭绝的危险。③我认为,对于因为失去栖息地而濒临灭绝的动物而言,动物园有必要存在来保护它们。

④在过去,纯粹为了供好奇的人类消遣而将野生动物关在小笼子里,人们往往认为这种做法很残忍。⑤许多人认为,应该让野生动物在其自然栖息地自由漫步,捕食天然的猎物。⑥我也认为这是最理想的,但不幸的是,由于地球上庞大的人口数量,许多动物的自然栖息地遭到破坏,许多野生动物的猎物数量已经不足以维持这些动物的生存。⑦城市、城镇和工业已经占据了曾经是各种不同物种栖息地的土地。

⑧因此，我同意这样的观点：为了保护和维系许多在野外几乎没有生存机会的物种，现在动物园有必要存在。⑨例如，中国的大熊猫是濒危物种，它们在动物园里成功得到培育，这从而有助于保持这个物种存活。⑩同样，老虎在动物园里生活后，数量也在增加，如今许多动物都是在圈养的情况下培育的。⑪理想情况下，动物园里动物的人造栖息地应该尽可能地复制它们的自然栖息地。⑫通常情况下，动物园里的熊猫生活区里有竹子，这样它们可以像在野外一样吃自己最喜欢的食物。

⑬总之，因为许多野生动物的自然栖息地遭到人类破坏，所以我们可以尽我们最大的努力在动物园里为它们提供尽可能宽敞和自然的人工环境，以便让许多濒危物种能够存活。

Test 4

①had advanced改为has advanced

②spoke改为speak

③understanding改为understand; communicating改为communicate

④getting改为get

⑤were改为was

⑥used改为had used; shares改为share

⑦had改为has

⑧conversing改为converse

⑨speak改为speaks

⑩communicating改为communicate

⑪did改为do

⑫believed改为believe

⑬teach改为be taught; communicating改为communicate

【译文】

①近年来，计算机技术有了显著的进步。②现在我们可以使用计算机翻译软件与讲不同语言的人交流。③尽管我们开发出了这些有用的资源，但我不同意孩子不应该学习外语的观点，因为学习另一种语言不仅可以帮助个人更好地理解母语，而且还可以帮助他们在个人和文化层面上进行交流。

④首先，学习一门外语通常有助于个人更好地深入了解自己的母语。⑤例如，从个人经验来看，我发现学习意大利语有助于我积累更多我的母语——西班牙语的词汇。⑥虽然计算机可以帮助将西班牙语翻译成意大利语，但如果我完全使用计算机为我翻译，我就不会进一步了解我的母语和其他语言，比如英语和德语，这两门语言之间也有一些相似的构词法。⑦这样一来，学习外语有很多好处，不仅限于交流。

⑧其次，尽管计算机翻译软件可以帮助人们翻译外语文本，甚至帮我们与讲不同语言的人交谈，但计算机无法在个人或文化层面上进行交流。⑨例如，我最亲密的一个朋友，他/她的母语是意大利语。⑩我们可以在计算机的帮助下进行对话，但当我们尝试真正开口与对方交流时，我们的对话更丰富、更有趣。⑪此外，我们还可以分享我们的文化和祖国不同的方面，分享我们当地菜肴的味道和我们当地方言特有的表达，这些都是我们的计算机无法做到的。

⑫总而言之，我不认为计算机翻译足以满足讲不同语言的人之间的交流需求。⑬我认为应该让孩子们学习外语，以拓宽他们的知识面，帮助他们与其他文化背景的人交流。

Test 5

①popularity; aspects　②overuse

③advantages; disadvantages　④lifestyle

⑤children　⑥Internet; business

⑦communication　⑧impacts

⑨content　⑩entertainment

⑪studies; research　⑫downsides

⑬conclusion

【译文】

①在过去的十年里，手机的普及率飞速增长，改变了人们生活方式的许多方面。②大多数人同意这些变化大多是积极的，但过度使用手机也有消极的一面。③在我看来，手机的优点多于缺点。

④手机的使用非常广泛，对普通人的生活方式产生了许多积极的影响。⑤手机让父母能够轻松与他们的孩子保持联系。⑥另外，现在很多人的手

机都可以上网，所以他们不仅可以用手机打电话，还可以通过手机发送电子邮件和开展业务。⑦这一点非常有好处，因为这意味着人们不必局限于在家里或办公室来与朋友、家人或商业伙伴取得联系；沟通可以在任何地点随时进行。

⑧然而，大量使用手机也会对个人和社会产生负面影响。⑨例如，如果儿童在无人看管的情况下使用手机，他们可能会在互联网上访问不适当的内容。⑩此外，与那些必须依靠社交活动来娱乐的人相比，过于依赖具有联网功能手机的人可能会变得更加孤僻。⑪一些研究还表明，过度使用手机会带来健康风险，如癌症，尽管还需要进行更多的研究来证明这一理论。⑫如果人们意识到使用手机的这些弊端，我相信他们可以采取措施，防止大多数社会和医疗问题的发生。

⑬总之，在我看来，手机的优点远远超过其缺点。

Test 6

①of; in ②into ③in; in
④In; in ⑤By; to; in ⑥at
⑦to ⑧By; to; after ⑨to; to
⑩to; by

【译文】

①该折线图显示了到新西兰旅游的外国游客的数量，以千人为单位。②该图分了十二个月。③总体而言，7月份游客数量最多，12月份和1月份游客数量最少。

④1月份，游客人数在1,000人左右，然后在整个2月份略有增加，3月份达到3,000人左右。⑤到4月份，新西兰的游客人数已上升到5,000人，并在5、6月份继续逐步增加，达到约7,000人。⑥从那时起，游客数量急剧增加，在7月份达到顶峰，约1.2万名游客，是所有月份中最高的。⑦7月份之后，游客数量在8月份减少到略高于1万人。⑧到了9月份，游客人数又略有增加，达到1.1万人左右，但在9月份之后又开始下降。⑨游客数量在10月份显著下降，只有7,000人左右，然后在11月份增加到8,000人。⑩在11月至12月期间，到新西兰旅游的游客数量大幅减少，到年底时降至2,000人左右。

Test 7

①show ②decreased; increased
④gradually; reaching ⑤topped
⑥ranged ⑧occurring
⑨fluctuated ⑩hovered; slightly

【译文】

①这两张柱状图显示了四个城市在四个不同年份的平均降雨量(毫米)和平均气温(摄氏度)。

②在第一张柱状图中，第一年圣保罗的平均降雨量最高，在2005年约760毫米，这一数值在2015年降至约600毫米，2020年再次增至约805毫米，是图中显示的最高降雨量。③墨西哥城也呈现出类似的趋势。④在意大利罗马，2005年降雨量最大(略低于500毫米)，然后在接下来的每一年数值逐渐减少，在2020年降雨量达到略低于300毫米。⑤纽约的年降雨量一直都排在第二位，除了在2015年位列榜首。⑥在其余三年中，数值范围在约600到775毫米之间。

⑦第二张柱状图显示了这四个城市的平均气温(摄氏度)。⑧在所显示的四个年份中，墨西哥城每年的平均气温都是最高的，其中最高气温为25摄氏度，出现在2015年。⑨在四个年份中，圣保罗和罗马的气温都在15至20摄氏度之间浮动。⑩然而，纽约的年气温最低，2005年至2015年的气温都在15摄氏度左右徘徊，然后在2020年略微上升到约17摄氏度。

Test 8

① This diagram shows **proportions of** different transactions **paid in** cash, **by** direct debit **card** and **by** credit card in each year from 2013 to 2023. ② There is a big difference **among** them.
③ **The percentage of transactions paid by** credit card was generally low **among these three** kinds of transactions but **rose** in 2022 and 2023 over **that of** cash **payment**. ④ **The percentage of transactions paid in** cash was highest at the beginning in 2013 and **got** smaller over time in **the** graph. ⑤ By 2023, **it had become**

the smallest. ⑥ It is around 10 percent of **all** transactions. ⑦ **The proportion of the** direct debit card **payment** was low in 2013 but not as low as **that of the** credit card **payments**. ⑧ It was getting higher overall and **from** 2018 to 2023 **had** surpassed **the percentages of the** credit card and cash **payments**. ⑨ On the whole, **the proportion of the** credit card **payment** remained relatively stable, **while the** direct debit card **proportion went** up and **the** cash **proportion fell down**.

【译文】

①这张图显示了从2013到2023年期间每一年使用现金、直接借记卡和信用卡支付的不同交易所占比例。②这些交易类型的比例存在很大差异。

③在这三种类型的交易中，由信用卡支付的交易比例总体上较低，但在2022年和2023年有所增加，高于现金支付的比例。④现金交易的比例在一开始2013年时最高，在图中随着时间的推移变得越来越小。⑤到了2023年，现金支付的比例变成了最小的。⑥它占所有交易的10%左右。⑦2013年，直接借记卡支付所占比例较低，但没有信用卡支付的比例低。⑧直接借记卡支付的比例总体一直在增加，并且在2018年到2023年超过了信用卡和现金支付的比例。⑨总的来看，信用卡支付的比例保持相对稳定，而直接借记卡的比例上升，现金的比例下降。

Test 9

① Tourism has become the main type of entertainment, so the number of tourists has increased rapidly in recent years. ② However, some people say that excessive number of tourists visiting old sites will damage the site and the quality of **the** tour will **be reduced**. ③ I strongly agree with this viewpoint.

④ Firstly, people **seek to discover different things** by themselves due to curiosity. ⑤ In old sites such as museums, there are lots of old and fragile things, **like** antiques **and artefacts**. ⑥ With large crowds of tourists, it is difficult for the tour-guide to tell the visitors what they should do and what they should not do. ⑦ **For that reason**, the **antiques** and **other protected objects** are **easily or** haphazardly damaged by the visitors. ⑧ Secondly, too many visitors also affect the quality of the tour. ⑨ The tourists are from everywhere **across the world**, so different language**s are** a big problem. ⑩ There **are** not enough well-informed tour-guides to instruct the tourists. ⑪ Additionally, to satisfy all the demands of the visitors is another **problem**. ⑫ For example, in one tour, one visitor wants to visit **for** long periods of time, but another feels hungry so he or she needs to enjoy their meals. ⑬ That causes difficulty for the tour-guide to organise and manage the tour.

⑭ One solution to decrease the negative effects of large crowds is to limit the number of visitors in one tour. ⑮ Another way is **introducing policies** to protect and conserve the **treasures** in old sites. ⑯ For example, do not allow the children **to** visit such these places or do not let the tourists touch the things in old sites. ⑰ With these **measures**, I believe the **damage** in old sites will decrease.

⑱ In summary, it can be seen that overcrowding of visitors can easily **damage** old sites and **detract from** the quality of **a** visit. ⑲ We should all try to make sure that this does not happen often in our tourism development.

【译文】

①旅游已成为人们主要的娱乐方式，因此近年来游客数量迅速增长。②然而，一些人说，过多的游客参观旧址会破坏旧址，降低旅行质量。③我非常同意这一观点。

④首先，出于好奇心，人们会自行去发现不同的东西。⑤在像博物馆这样历史悠久的地方，有很多古老而脆弱的物品，比如古董和工艺品。⑥由于游客人数众多，导游很难告诉游客应该做什么，不应该做什么。⑦因此，古董和其他受保护的物品很容

易或不经意地被游客破坏。⑧其次，游客太多也会影响旅行的质量。⑨游客来自世界各地，所以语言不通是一个大问题。⑩没有足够多见多识广的导游来指导游客。⑪此外，要满足游客的所有需求也是一个问题。⑫例如，在同一个团里，一位游客想要长时间参观，但另一位游客感到饥肠辘辘因此需要用餐。⑬这给导游组织和管理行程带来了困难。

⑭要减少人潮的负面影响，一个解决方法是限制旅行团的游客数量。⑮另一个方法是出台政策保护和保存旧址的宝物。⑯例如，不允许儿童参观这些地方或不让游客触摸旧址中的物品。⑰有了这些措施，我相信对旧址的破坏将会减少。

⑱总而言之，可以看出，游客太多很容易破坏旧址，并降低游览质量。⑲我们都应该努力确保这种情况在我们的旅游业发展中不会经常发生。

Test 10

① In the modern world, most students use the computers **widely** for the education, and people believe that teachers play **a** less important role in **the** classroom. ② I disagree with this. ③ I would like to talk about computer in education. ④ These days, **many people** are very busy **with schoolwork**. ⑤ After school, they usually **continue studying independently**. ⑥ Under these circumstances, they do not have spare time so that they cannot enjoy **leisure** activities. ⑦ All they do is study. ⑧ For **that** reason, using the computer **in** education is very helpful for students. ⑨ Computer education systems **often help students do their work more quickly because students can easily access information they need**. ⑩Moreover, **computerised information systems** are **often** more extensive than school **library** systems. ⑪For these reasons, most students prefer to use the computer to learn.

⑫ **On the other hand**, some people worry **about** computers **in** education as students often **spend too much time on computers**. ⑬ **For example, students may be tempted to play computer games, send e-mails, browse entertainment sites and use chat rooms**. ⑭ Some people say that nowadays students **have too much exposure to computerised** communication, **which may waste time they should spend on study**. ⑮ **Therefore**, the teacher's role **has become even** more important than before. ⑯ Teachers **need to be in control of** their students and encourage **them to focus on** their **study**.

【译文】

①在现代社会，大多数学生广泛使用计算机进行教育学习，人们认为教师在课堂上发挥的作用没那么重要了。②我不同意这一观点。

④现在很多人的学业都很繁忙。⑤放学后，他们通常继续独立学习。⑥在这种情况下，他们没有闲暇时间，因此无法享受休闲活动。⑦他们所做的一切就是学习。⑧因此，在教育中使用计算机对学生来说是非常有帮助的。⑨计算机教育系统往往能帮助学生更快地完成任务，因为他们可以轻松获取需要的信息。⑩此外，计算机信息系统储存的信息通常比学校图书馆系统的更全面。⑪出于这些原因，大多数学生更喜欢使用计算机学习。

⑫另一方面，有些人对计算机用于教育表示担心，因为学生经常花过多时间在计算机上。⑬例如，学生可能会受到引诱，玩计算机游戏、发电子邮件、浏览娱乐网站和使用聊天室。⑭有人说，现在的学生过多地使用计算机来交流，可能会浪费他们本来用于学习的时间。⑮因此，教师的作用变得比以前更重要了。⑯教师需要控制学生并鼓励他们专注于自己的学业。

读者意见反馈卡

《雅思语法》

读者个人资料

姓　　名:＿＿＿＿＿＿　　性　别:□男　　□女　　电　话:＿＿＿＿＿＿

院系年级:＿＿＿＿＿＿　　Email:＿＿＿＿＿＿

通讯地址:＿＿＿＿＿＿＿＿＿＿＿＿＿＿＿＿＿＿＿＿＿＿

您购买过几本华研图书?

□1本　　　　　　　　□2-3本　　　　　　　□4本及以上

促使您购买本书的因素(可多选)

□封面、装帧设计　　　□封面、封底文字　　　□价格

□同学、朋友的评价　　□前言和目录　　　　　□作者或出版社的名声

□老师推荐　　　　　　□编排逻辑　　　　　　□买过华研其他书,感觉满意

□其他＿＿＿＿＿＿＿＿＿＿＿＿＿＿＿＿＿＿＿＿＿＿＿＿＿

您对本书封面设计的满意度:

□很满意　　　　　　　□满意　　　　　　　　□一般

您对本书印刷质量的满意度:

□很满意　　　　　　　□满意　　　　　　　　□一般

您对本书的总体满意度:

□很满意　　　　　　　□满意　　　　　　　　□一般

您是从何处购买到本书的?

□书店　　　　　　　　□网络　　　　　　　　□师兄师姐

本书最令您满意的是:

□讲解模式　　　　　　□长难句分析　　　　　□答案解析

□词汇注释　　　　　　□译文精准　　　　　　□视频学习

□其他＿＿＿＿＿＿＿＿＿＿＿＿＿＿＿＿＿＿＿＿＿＿＿＿＿

您看到本书还有哪些校对错漏?

＿＿＿＿＿＿＿＿＿＿＿＿＿＿＿＿＿＿＿＿＿＿＿＿＿＿＿＿

您希望本书在哪些方面进行改进?

＿＿＿＿＿＿＿＿＿＿＿＿＿＿＿＿＿＿＿＿＿＿＿＿＿＿＿＿

您还读过市面上哪些同类书?这些书哪些特点吸引您?

＿＿＿＿＿＿＿＿＿＿＿＿＿＿＿＿＿＿＿＿＿＿＿＿＿＿＿＿

您对华研外语的建议或要求:

＿＿＿＿＿＿＿＿＿＿＿＿＿＿＿＿＿＿＿＿＿＿＿＿＿＿＿＿